EDINBURGH

ESTATE PUBLICATIONS
Bridewell House,
Tenterden, Kent.
TN30 6EP
Tel: 01580 764225

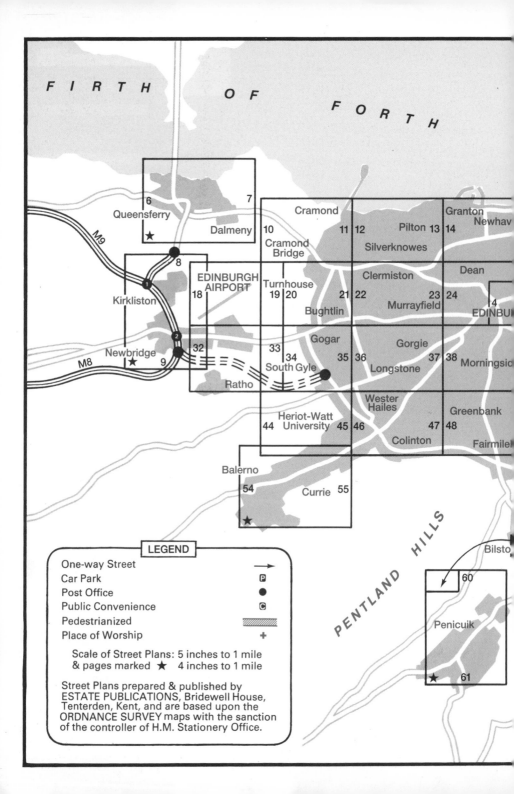

ESTATE PUBLICATIONS

EDINBURGH

QUEENSFERRY · KIRKLISTON · PENICUIK · DALKEITH
NEWTONGRANGE · TRANENT · COCKENZIE

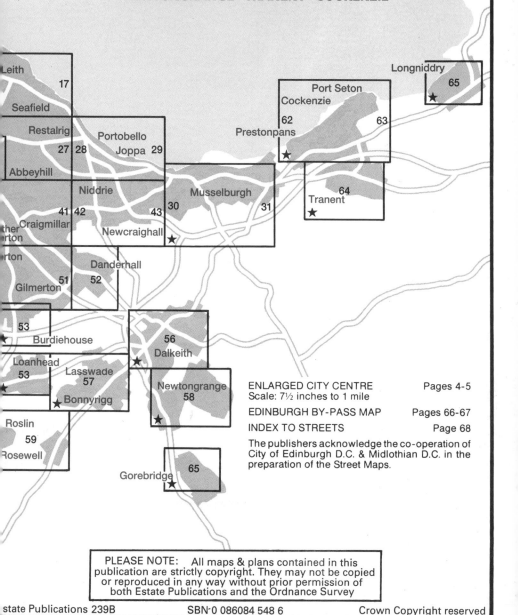

ENLARGED CITY CENTRE   Pages 4-5
Scale: 7½ inches to 1 mile

EDINBURGH BY-PASS MAP   Pages 66-67

INDEX TO STREETS   Page 68

The publishers acknowledge the co-operation of City of Edinburgh D.C. & Midlothian D.C. in the preparation of the Street Maps.

state Publications 239B   SBN·0 086084 548 6   Crown Copyright reserved

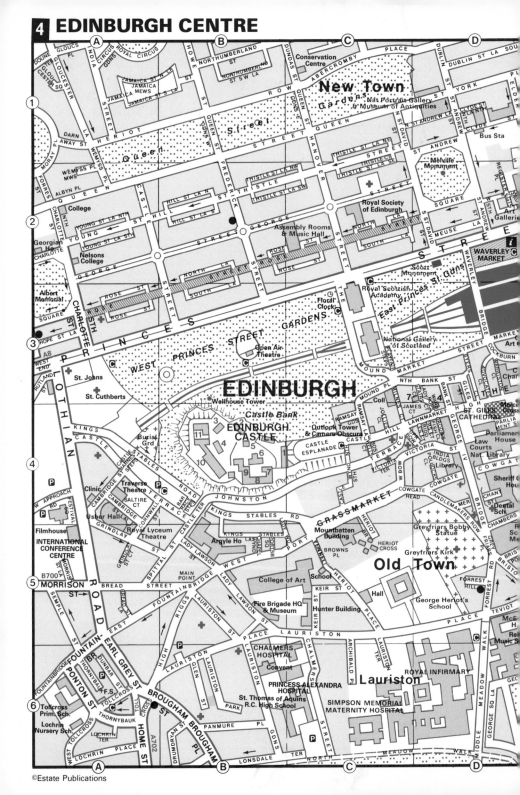

EDINBURGH

EDINBURGH CASTLE

New Town

Old Town

Lauriston

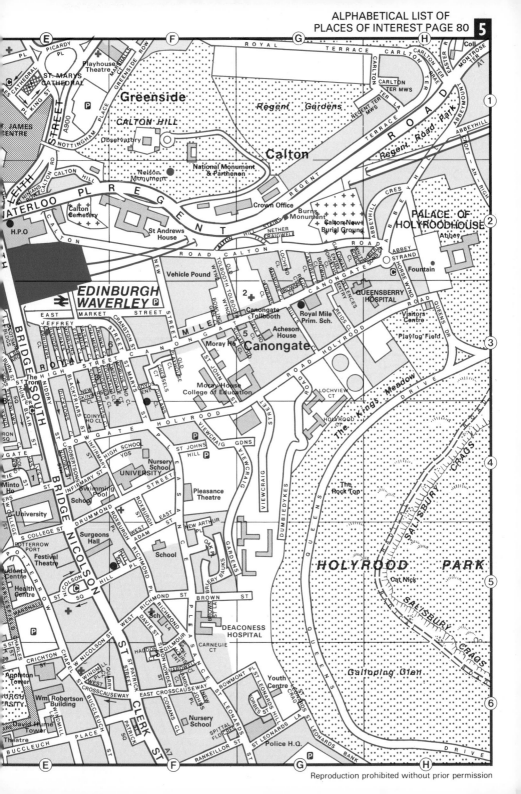

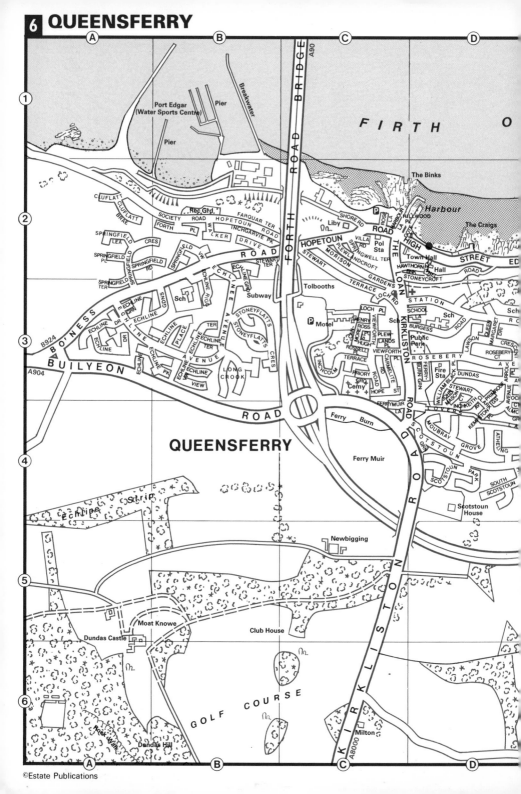

FIRTH O

Port Edgar
(Water Sports Centre)
Pier
Pier
Breakwater
The Binks
Harbour
Hillwood
The Craigs

CLUFLATT
CLUFLATT BRAE
SOCIETY
ROAD
Rec Grd.
FARQUAR TER
HOPETOUN ROAD
FORTH PL
INCHGARVIE PK
WALKER DRIVE
SPRINGFIELD LEA
SPRINGFIELD CRES
SPRINGFIELD PL
SPRINGFIELD RD
SPRINGFIELD WY
SPRINGFIELD TER
STEWART TER
ECHLINE GRN
ECHLINE RIGG
Sch
ROAD
STEWART
Shore Rd
Liby
HOPETOUN ROAD
Town Hall
Hall
STREET
HIGH
Stoneycroft
Hawthorn
VILLA RD
Pol Sta
SPRINGWELL TER
PLEWLANDCROFT
MORISON
GARDENS
TERRACE
STONEYCROFT

B924
BO'NESS
BUILYEON
A904
ECHLINE
ECHLINE DR
ECHLINE GDNS
ECHLINE PLACE
ECHLINE TER
ECHLINE AVENUE
ECHLINE PK
ECHLINE
ECHLINE VIEW
AVENUE
LONG CROOK
STONEYFLATTS
STONEYFLATTS CRES
Subway
Tolbooths
Motel
HENRY ROSS PL
HUGH RUSSELL PL
LINCOLN
VIEWFORTH
PLEW LANDS
CARMELITE
PRIORY ROAD
Cemy
HOPE ST
FERRYMUIR LA
TERRACE
LOCH RD
LOCH PL
STATION
SCHOOL
Sch
Sch
BURGESS
Public Park
ROSEBERY
LAWSON
BURN GRN
FERRY
Fire Sta
DUNDAS
STEWART
MARGARET DRI
ROSEBERY CT
CRES
RO
QUEEN
AVE
WILLIAM BLACK PL
KEITH CT
INCH KEITH CT
KEMP PL
STEWART PL
PRIMROSE PL
ARROL
AVENUE
ALMO
ATHEN
ROAD

QUEENSFERRY

Ferry Burn
Ferry Muir
SCOTSTOUN
MOUBRAY GRN
SCOTSTOUN GRN
PARK
SOUTH SCOTSTOUN
Scotstoun House

Strip
Echline
Newbigging
KIRKLISTON ROAD

Moat Knowe
Dundas Castle
Club House

GOLF COURSE

Rec Wlk
Dundas Hill
Milton
A8000

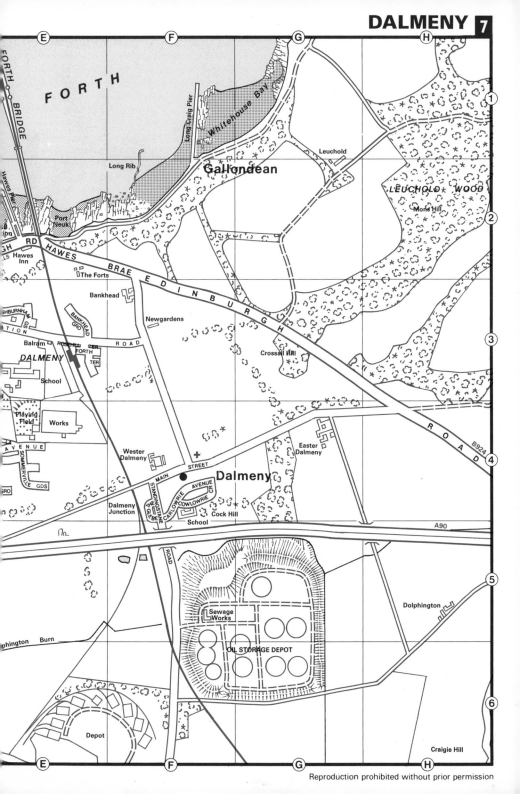

FORTH BRIDGE

F O R T H

Long Craig Pier

Whitehouse Bay

Long Rib

Gallondean

Leuchold

LEUCHOLD WOOD

Mons Hill

Port Neuk

GH RD

Hawes Pier

HAWES

Hawes Inn

BRAE

The Forts

Bankhead

EDINBURGH

BANKHEAD GRO

Newgardens

SHBURNHAM GDS

TION

ROAD

Balram

ROSEHILL

FORTH

TER

DALMENY

TER

Crossall Hill

School

Playing Field

Works

AVENUE

SOMMERVILLE GDS

GRO

Wester Dalmeny

STREET

Dalmeny

Easter Dalmeny

R O A D

B924

Dalmeny Junction

MAIN

THE STANDINGSTANE GLEBE

CARLOWRIE

COWLOWRIE

AVENUE

Cock Hill

School

A90

OIL STORAGE DEPOT

Sewage Works

ROAD

Dolphington

phington Burn

Depot

Craigie Hill

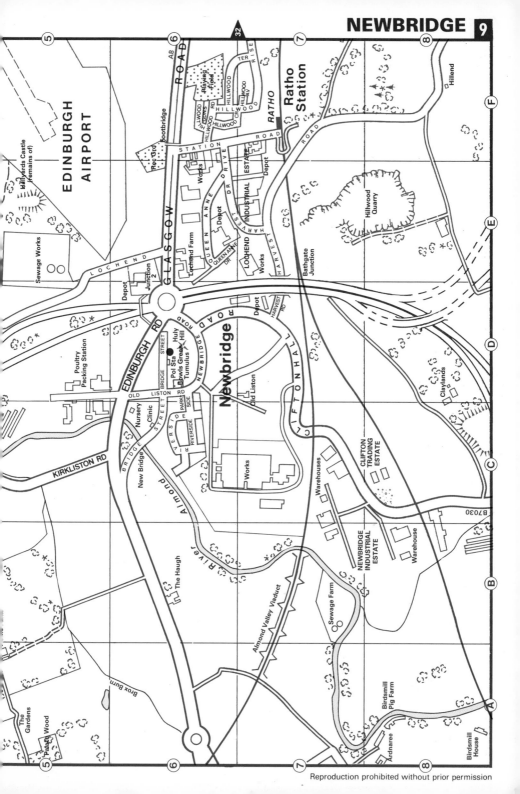

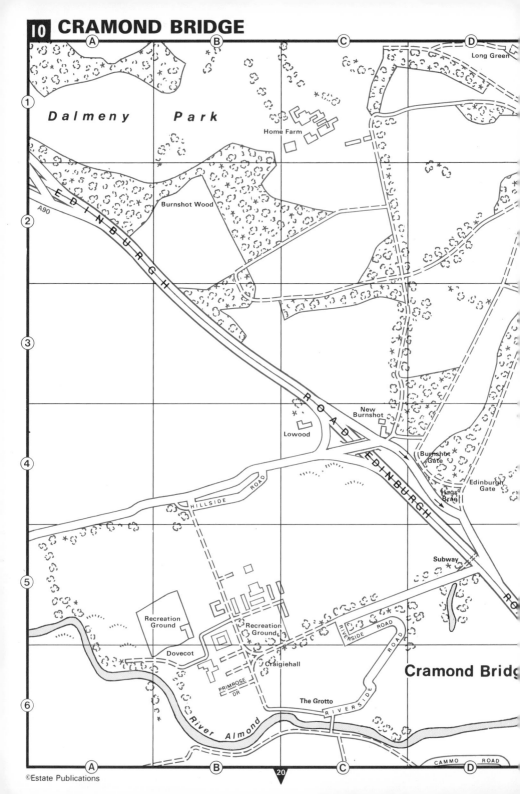

Long Green

Dalmeny Park

Home Farm

A90

Burnshot Wood

ROAD

New Burnshot

Lowood

Burnshot Gate

EDINBURGH

Edinburgh Gate

Hags Brae

HILLSIDE ROAD

Subway

Recreation Ground

Recreation Ground

RIVERSIDE ROAD

Cramond Bridg

Dovecot

Craigiehall

PRIMROSE DR

The Grotto

RIVERSIDE

River Almond

CAMMO ROAD

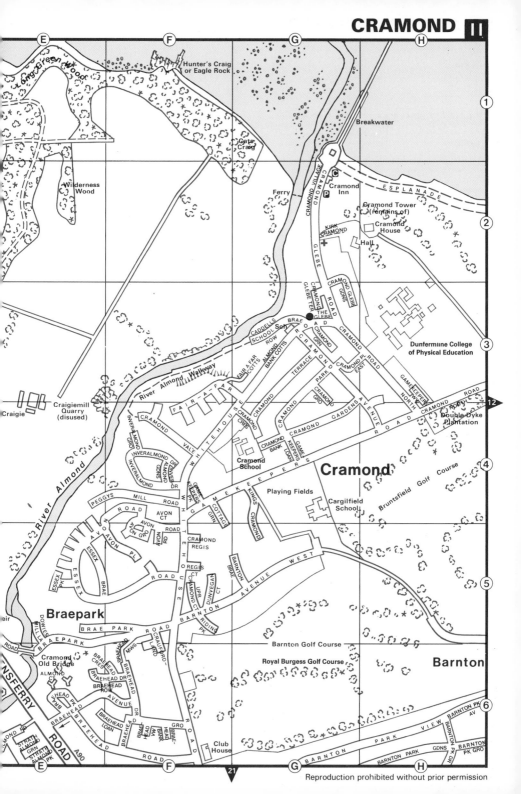

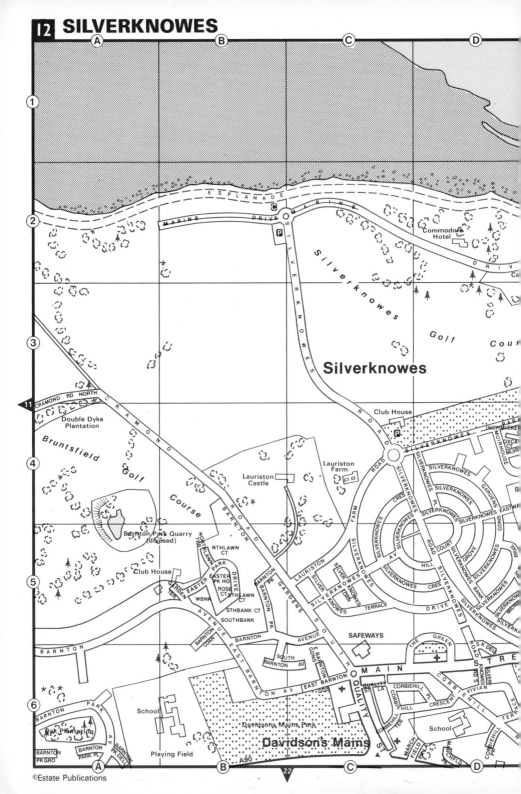

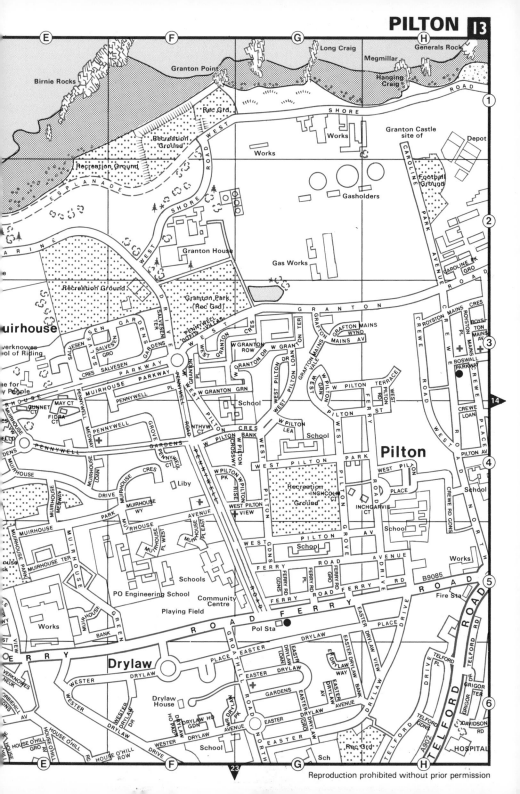

Birnie Rocks
Granton Point
Long Craig
Megmillar
Generals Rock
Hanging Craig
SHORE ROAD
Rec Grd.
Granton Castle
site of
Depot
Works
Works
Caroline Park
Football Ground
Gasholders
Granton House
Gas Works
Recreation Ground
Recreation Ground
Esplanade
West Shore Road
Granton Park (Rec Grd)
Muirhouse
GRANTON ROAD
Gunnet Ct
Fidra Ct
May Ct
Medway
Pennywell
Salvesen Gardens
Salvesen Gro
Salvesen Cres
Muirhouse Parkway
Pennywell PL
Pennywell Road
W Granton Row
W Granton Grn
W Granton Dr
W Granton Ter
Grafton Mains Wynd
Grafton Mains Av
W Pilton Ter
Royston Mains Cres
Royston Mains PL
Boswall Pky
Crewe Road West
Crewe Loan
Pilton Av
Caroline Pk Gro
School
W Pilton Lea
School
W Pilton Crossway
W Pilton Pk
W Pilton Rise
West Pilton View
Bank
Inchcolm Ct
Inchgarvie Ct
West Pilton Place
Pilton Av
School
School
Muirhouse Way
Muirhouse Medway
Muirhouse Drive
Muirhouse Park
Muirhouse PL West
Muirhouse PL East
Muirhouse Avenue
Liby
Recreation Ground
West Gdns
Pilton Grove
School
Ferry Rd Gdns
Ferry Road
Ferry PL
Ferry Rd Grdn
Avenue
Avenue Drive
Crewe Rd Gdns
School
Works
B9085
Fire Sta
PO Engineering School
Community Centre
Playing Field
Works
Muirhouse Bank
Pol Sta
FERRY ROAD
Drylaw
Drylaw House
Wester Drylaw
Easter Drylaw
Easter Drylaw Loan
Easter Drylaw Gardens
Easter Drylaw View
Easter Drylaw Bank
Easter Drylaw Av
Easter Drylaw Avenue
Easter Drylaw Gro
Telford Drive
Telford PL
Grigor Ter
Grigor Gdns
Davidson Rd
Telford Road
Hospital
House O'Hill Gro
House O'Hill Row
Wester Drylaw Drive
School
Rec Grd
Sch
Groathill Road

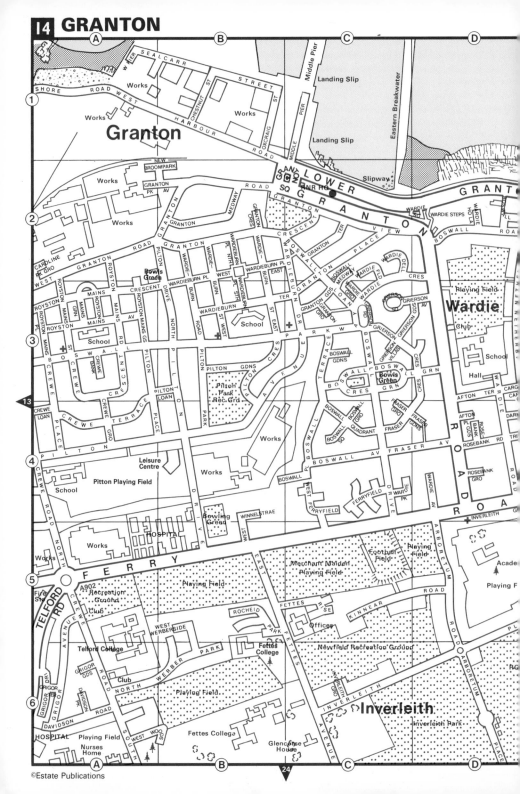

©Estate Publications

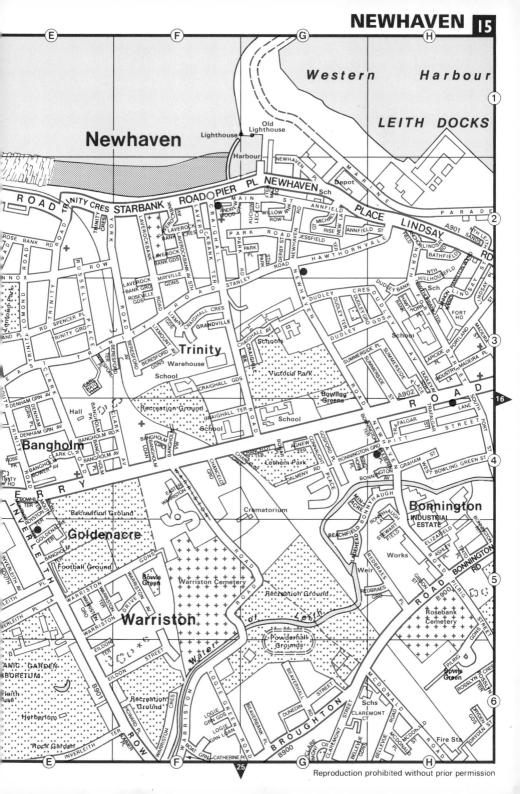

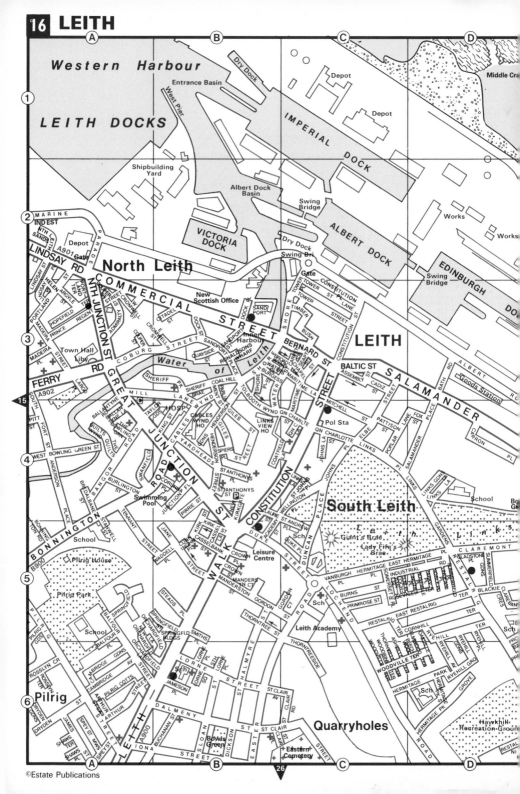

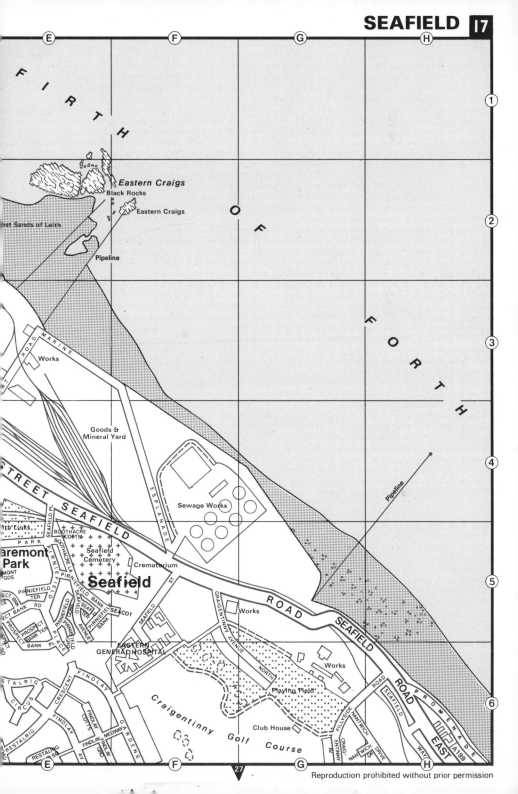

F I R T H   O F   F O R T H

Eastern Craigs
Black Rocks
Eastern Craigs
st Sands of Leith
Pipeline

MARINE ROAD
Works

Goods &
Mineral Yard

ESPLANADE

SEAFIELD STREET
SEAFIELD PL

Sewage Works

BOOTHACRE
COTTS
PIRNIEFIELD PLACE
Seafield
Cemetery
Crematorium

Seafield

th Links
PARK
aremont
Park
MONT
GDS
PIRNIEFIELD TER
PROSPECT BANK
PROSPECT BANK RD
PROSPECT BANK TER
PROSPECT BANK PL
PIRNIEFIELD GDNS
PIRNIEFIELD BANK
SEAFIELD AVENUE
SEAFIELD BANK
SEACOT
SEAFIELD ST

Works

EASTERN
GENERAL HOSPITAL

CRAIGENTINNY AVENUE

ROAD   SEAFIELD

Pipeline

Works

RESTALRIG CIRCUS
RESTALING
FINDLAY CRESCENT
FINDLAY COTTS
FINDLAY GARDENS
FINDLAY AV
MEDWAY

Craigentinny Golf Course

NORTH

Playing Field

Club House

FILLYSIDE ROAD
NANTWICH
CRAIGENTINNY AV
NANTWICH DRIVE
CRAIG-ENTINNY
WAY
SEAFIELD ROAD
PROMENADE
ROAD
EAST
A199

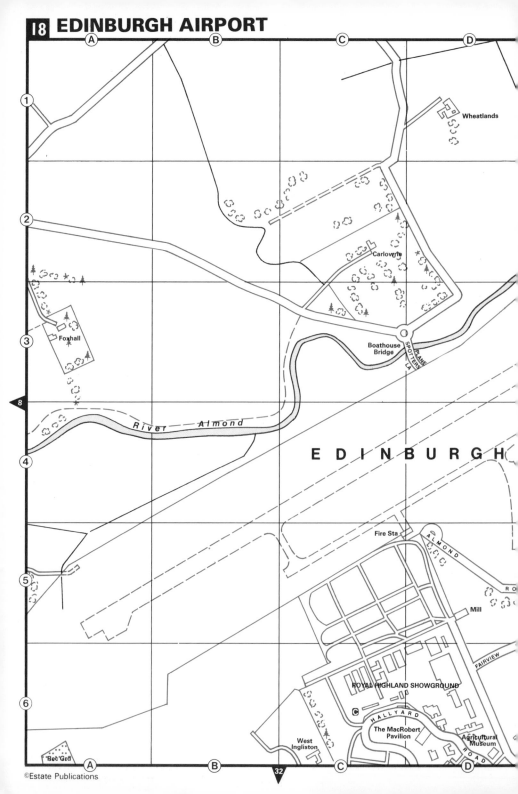

Wheatlands

Carlowrie

Foxhall

Boathouse
Bridge

PLANE SPOTTERS LA

River Almond

EDINBURGH

Fire Sta

ALMOND ROAD

Mill

FAIRVIEW

ROYAL HIGHLAND SHOWGROUND

HALLYARD

The MacRobert
Pavilion

Agricultural
Museum

ROAD

West
Ingliston

Rec Grd

E F 10 G H

Nether Lennie

1

Old Curling
Pond

River Almond

2

CAMMO ROAD

Turnhouse

Turnhouse

LENNYMUIR

Playing Field

TURNHOUSE

LENNYMUIR

FARM ROAD

3

20

(S C O T L A N D) A I R P O R T

4

MINAL
DINGS

i

P

JUBILEE ROAD

P

Cogar Burn

P

JUBILEE

ND AV

Pol Sta

EASTFIELD ROAD

5

IEW

ROAD

Gogar Mains

GOGAR MAINS FARM ROAD

Port-Royel
Golf Driving Range

Castle Gogar

Mains of Ingliston
(Smallholdings)

East Ingliston
House

ROAD

Castle Gogar
Gardens

6

E F 33 G H

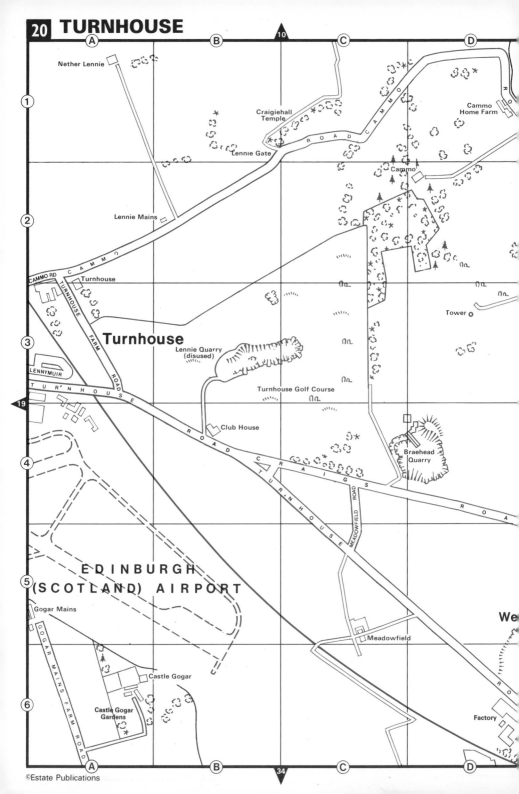

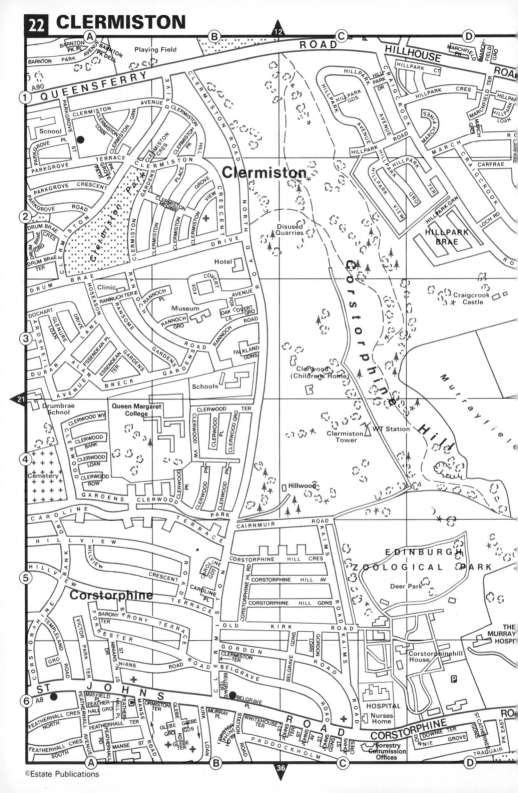

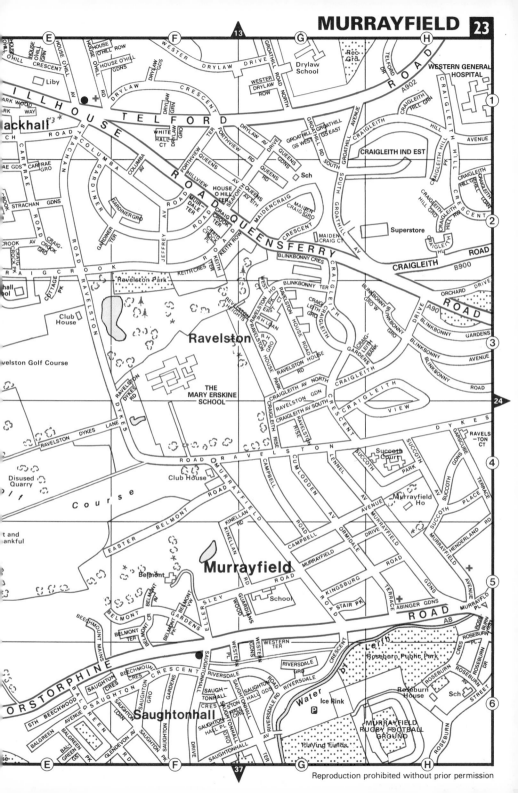

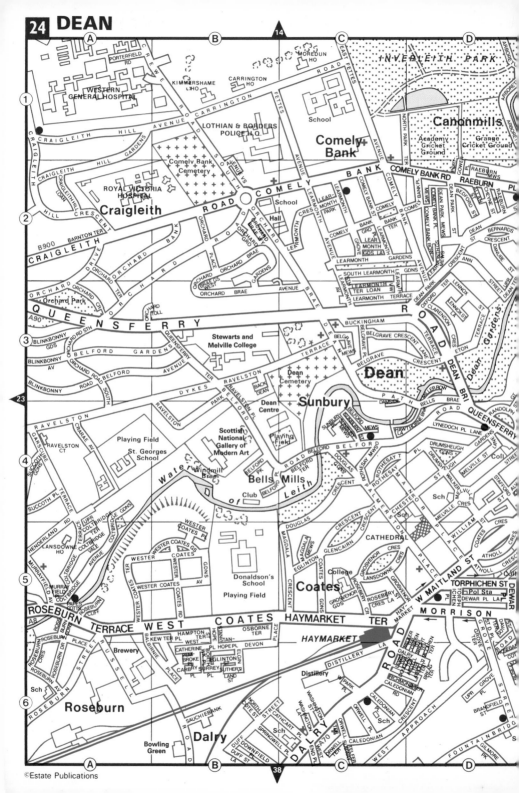

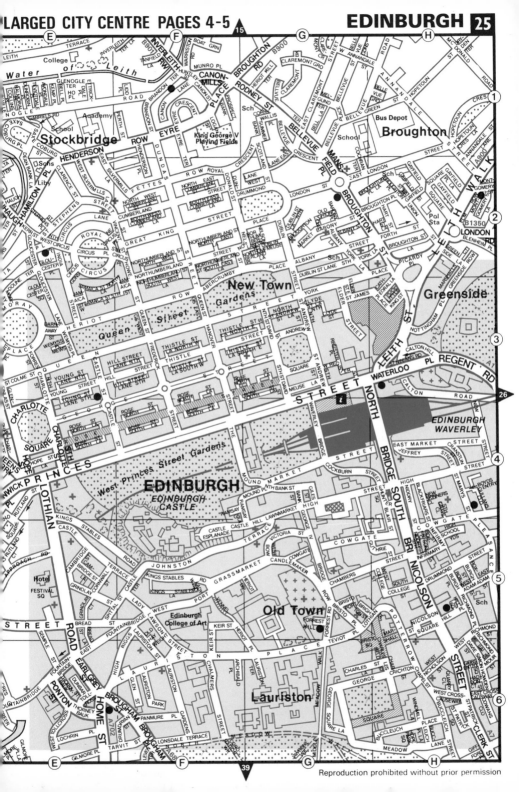

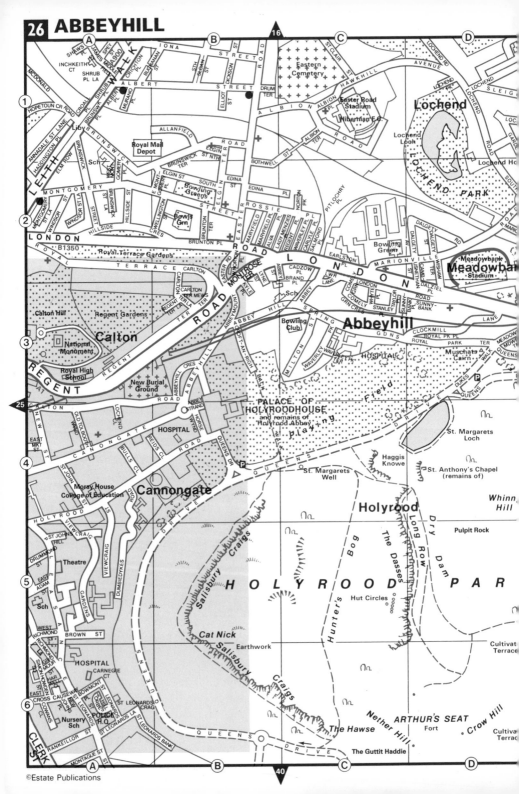

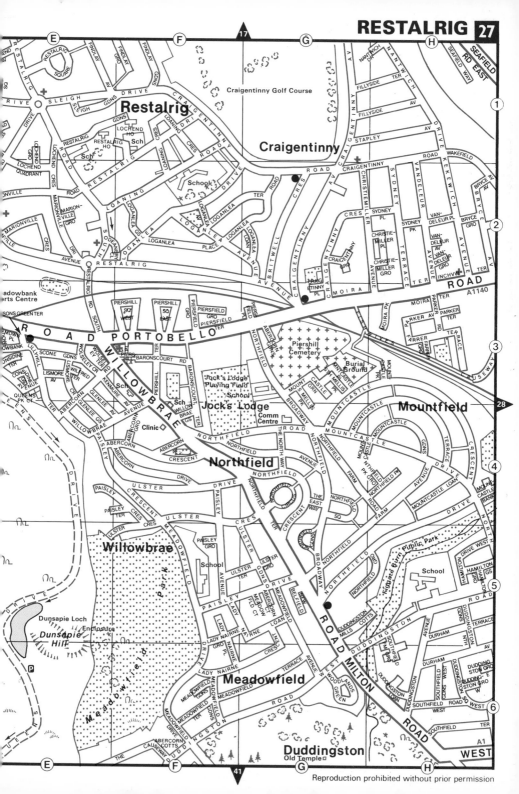

Craigentinny Golf Course

Restalrig

Craigentinny

Meadowbank
Sports Centre

R O A D   P O R T O B E L L O

Piersfield

Piersfield
Cemetery

Jock's Lodge
Playing Field

Jock's Lodge

Clinic

Comm
Centre

Northfield

Mountfield

Willowbrae

Dunsapie Loch

Enclosure

Dunsapie Hill

School

Meadowfield

Duddingston
Old Temple

M I L T O N   R O A D

WEST

A1

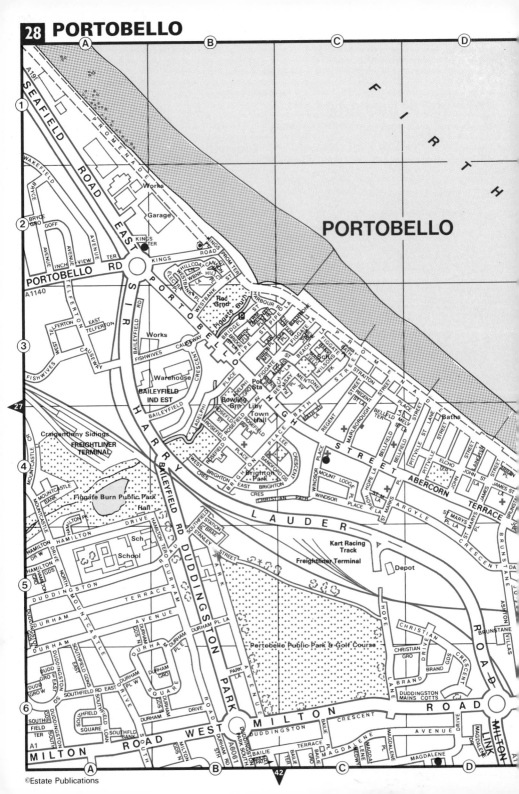

PORTOBELLO

FIRTH

SEAFIELD ROAD EAST

A1 9

PROMENADE

Works

Garage

WAKEFIELD

BRYCE

PRYCE

GOFF

AVENUE

AVENUE

INCH VIEW

TELFERTON

PORTOBELLO RD
A1140

EAST TELFERTON

WEST TELFERTON

TER

SIR

KINGS TER

KINGS ROAD

KINGS PROM TER

MILLCO4

WBNK PL

WESTBANK LA

WESTBANK

CANON

West bank

HARBOUR RD

PROMENADE

Rec Grnd

Figgate Burn

Bridge

FISHWIVES

CAUSEWAY

Works

FISHWIVES

CAUSEWAY

BAILEYFIELD RD

BAILEYFIELD

Warehouse

BAILEYFIELD
IND EST

PORTOBELLO

HIGH

CRESCENT

PLACE

ADELPHI

ROSEFIELD

ROSEFIELD

PLACE

Pol
Sta

ADELPHI
PL

Bowling Grn

Liby

Town
Hall

ROSEFIELD AV

FIGGATE

PIPE

PIPE

PIPE

ST

FIGGATE

BEACH

RAMSAY

MELV

MENTONE

BEACH LA

FIGGATE

WILSONS

PK

STRAITON

STREET

REGENT

BELLFLD

TER LA

STREET

MARLBOROUGH

HOPE

LA

MARKS

ST

REGENT

PITTVILLE

ELCHO

BELLFIELD

ST LA

BELLFIELD

ST

STREET

PITTVILLE

ST LA

Baths

ABERCORN
TERRACE

27

Craigentinny Sidings
FREIGHTLINER
TERMINAL

MOUNTCASTLE CR

MOUNTCASTLE
BANK

Figgate Burn Public Park

Hall

MOUNTCASTLE

MTH

HAMILTON

HAMILTON DR N

HAMILTON
DRIVE

HAMILTON TERR

DURHAM

Sch

School

SOUTHFIELD
ST

STATION

BRAE

STANLEY

STREET

PARK

DUDDINGSTON

STREET

WEST
CRES

BRIGHTON
HIGH

BRIGHTON
EAST

Brighton
Park

ROSEFIELD

PLACE

SANDFORD

Brighton

CRES

GS

CRESCENT

CHRISTIAN
PATH

WINDSOR PLACE

MOUNT LODGE

WINDSOR

PLACE

HOPE LA

ST MKS
PL LA

ARGYLE

ST MARYS
PL LA

MARLBOROUGH

JOHN ST LA

JOHN LA

JAMES ST LA

JAMES ST

ABERCORN

BRUNSTANE

CRESCENT

LAUDER

Kart Racing
Track
Freightliner Terminal

Depot

ROAD

HOPE

LANE

DRIVE

BRAND

CHRISTIAN
GRO

CHRISTIAN
CRESCENT

BRUNSTANE

ROAD

BRUNSTANE
VILLAS

ASHTON

DA
JO

DUDDINGSTON

DUDDINGSTON

DUDDINGSTON

TERRACE

AVENUE

DURHAM

DURHAM

DURHAM TERR

DURHAM

GRO

DURHAM PL LA

DURHAM PL W

Portobello Public Park & Golf Course

PARK

AVENUE

PARK

LA

BRAND

DUDDINGSTON
MAINS COTTS

CHRISTIAN
GRO

MILTON
LINK

SOUTHFIELD
ST

SOUTHFIELD
GDNS

SOUTHFIELD
RD EAST

DUDD
GRO EAST

DUDD
GRO W

SOUTH
FIELD
TER

DUDDINGSTON

SOUTHFIELD
SQUARE

Southfield
Square

SOUTHFIELD
BANK

SOUTHFLD
GDS N

DURHAM
SQUARE

DURHAM
GDS

DURHAM

DRIVE

MILTON ROAD WEST
A6061

DUDDINGSTON
PARK SOUTH

DUDDINGSTON

MILTON

BAILIE

BAILIE
TERRACE

MAGDALENE

PL

MAGDALENE
MEDWY

MAGDA

CRESCENT

AVENUE

Magdalene

MILTON
LINK

MAGDALENE
DR

A1

MILTON ROAD SOUTH
A1

42

©Estate Publications

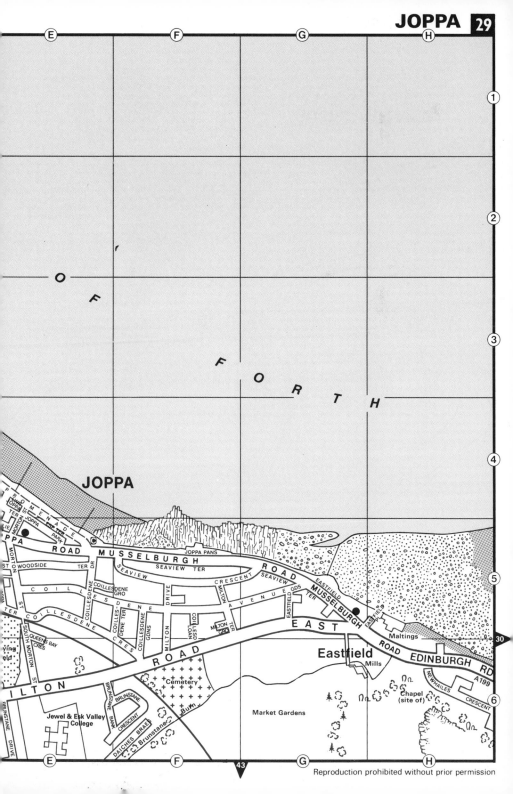

E · F · G · H

O F

F O R T H

JOPPA

PROMENADE ST

MORTON ST

JOPPA PARK

ROAD

MUSSELBURGH

ROAD

WOODSIDE

COILLESDENE

SEAVIEW

JOPPA PANS

SEAVIEW TER

CRESCENT

SEAVIEW

COLLESDENE GRO

DRIVE

MILTON TER

AVENUE

EASTFIELD GDNS

EASTFIELD GDS

MUSSELBURGH

ROAD

EASTFIELD

COILLESDENE TER

COILLESDENE DENE TER

COILLESDENE GDNS

MILTON LOAN

MILTON CRO

COILLESDENE CRES

MILTON

ROAD

EAST

ROAD EDINBURGH RD

Maltings

A199

Eastfield

Mills

QUEENS BAY CRES

SOUTH MORTON ST

ying eld

BRUNSTANE BANK

BRUNSTANE CRESCENT

Cemetery

Brunstane Burn

DAICHES BRAES

Brunstane

Chapel (site of)

NEWHAILES CRESCENT

Jewel & Esk Valley College

MILTON

BRUNSTANE DRIVE

Market Gardens

E · F · G · H

30 ▶

1
2
3
4
5
6

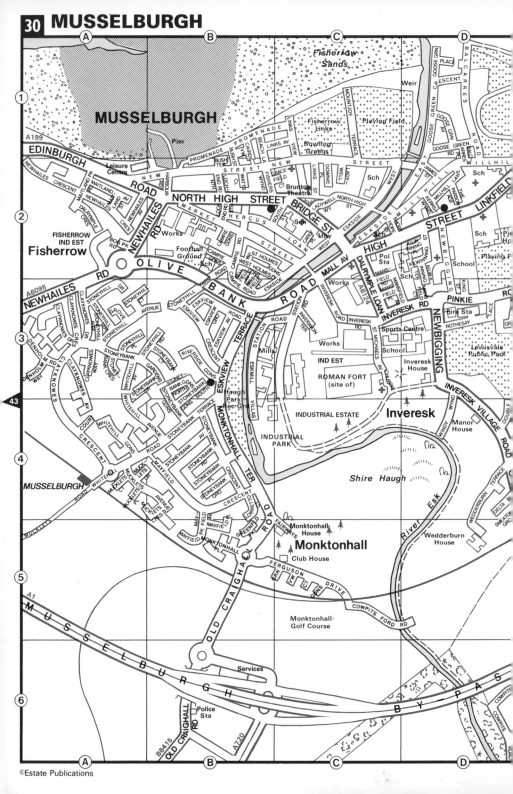

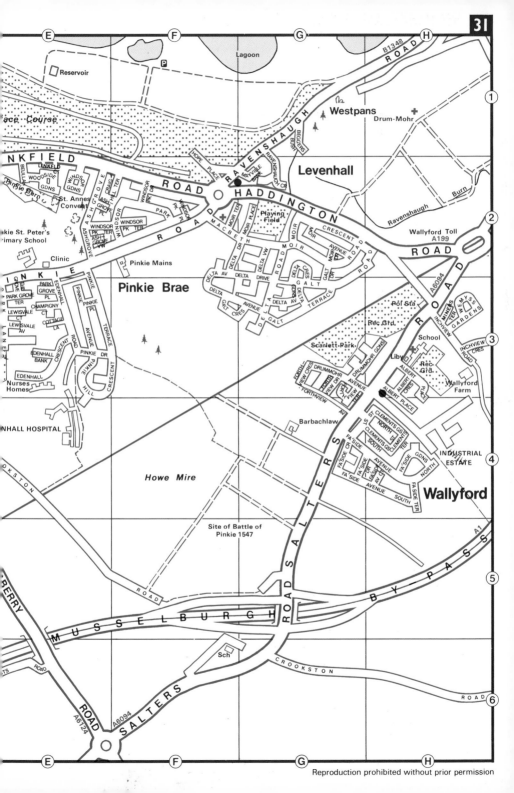

Reservoir

Lagoon

B1348 ROAD

E   F   G   H

Westpans

Drum-Mohr

ace Course

NKFIELD

LINKFIELD

BEULLALY

WOODSIDE GDNS

Pinkie Burn

W'DSOR GDNS

ASH GROVE PL

CRAIGHALL TER

WINDSOR PK DR

ORANGE

St. Annes Convent

kie St. Peter's imary School

ASHGROVE

WINDSOR PK TER

WINDSOR PK TER

ASHGROVE

WINDSOR PK VW

PARK

HADDINGTON ROAD

RAVENSHAUGH

HOPE PLACE

MAYVILLE PK

RAVENSHAUGH CR

BEGGES BUSH

Levenhall

Ravenshaugh

Burn

Clinic

Pinkie Mains

ROAD

MACBETH

MOIR TER

MOIR PLACE

Playing Field

CRESCENT

AVENUE

MOIR CRES

MOIR

GALT

GALT DR

ROAD

Wallyford Toll A199

ROAD

A6094

A6094 ROAD

Pinkie Brae

INKIE

PARK GROVE TER

EDENHALL

CHAMPIGNY CT

LEWISVALE CT

LEWISVALE AV

PINKIE GROVE

PINKIE PL

DELTA AV

DELTA

DELTA VW

DELTA DRIVE

DELTA AV

DELTA TERRACE

DELTA AV

GALT CRES

DELTA GALT

AVENUE

Pol Sta

Rec Grd.

School

MINERS

INCHVIEW

WEMYSS GARDENS

INCHVIEW CRES

INCHVIEW ROAD

Scarlett Park

Lib

Rec Grd.

EDENHALL BANK

CRESCENT

PINKIE

PINKIE DR

PINKIE AVENUE

PINKIE TERRACE

ALBERT PLACE

ALBERT CRES

Wallyford Farm

EDENHALL

Nurses Homes

HILL CRESCENT

FORTH VIEW

DRUMMOHR

VIEW DR

DRUMMOHR GDNS

DRUMMOHR AVENUE

FORTHVIEW

VIEW

ALBERT PLACE

NHALL HOSPITAL

Barbachlaw

ST. CLEMENTS GDNS NORTH

ST. CLEMENTS TER

ST. CLEMENTS GDNS

ST. CLEMENTS SOUTH

FA'SIDE CR

FA'SIDE DR

FA'SIDE AVENUE

FA'SIDE GDNS NORTH

FA'SIDE TER

FA'SIDE AVENUE SOUTH

SALTERS

INDUSTRIAL ESTATE

Wallyford

Howe Mire

Site of Battle of Pinkie 1547

OKSTON

ROAD

SALTERS ROAD

MUSSELBURGH

BY-PASS

A1

Sch

CROOKSTON

ROAD

ERRY

TS

ROAD

SALTERS

ROAD

A6124

A6094

E   F   G   H

1   2   3   4   5   6

Reproduction prohibited without prior permission

Rec Grd
Footbridge
West Ingliston
A8
HALLYARD ROAD
GLASGOW
Works
HILLWOOD GDS
Playing Field
R
O
A
QUEEN ANNE
HARVEST DRIVE
HILLWOOD ROAD
HILLWOOD CRES
RD
HILLWOOD TER
HILLWOOD AV
HILLWOOD RISE
Ratho Station
Depot
Primary School
HARVEST
STATION ROAD
RATHO
Norton M
Norton Hotel
Hillwood Quarry
BAIRD ROAD
Hillend
Ratho Byres
ROAD
Freelands
Works
FREELANDS
Burial Ground
Hall
Ratho Hall
Kirkten Farm
BAIRD ROAD
UNION
CANAL
HALLCROFT GDN
HALLCROFT NEUK
HALLCROFT
HALL-CROFT
HALLCROFT CL
HALLCROFT RISE
HALLCROFT PARK
CRAIGPARK
CRAIGPARK AVENUE
CRAIGPARK CRES
NORTH
SCHOOL WYND
STREET
MAIN
ROAD
WEST
CROFT
EAS
CROFT
Ratho P Garden
R
O
A
Bowling Green
Playing Field
PARK
Bridge Inn
BAIRD ROAD
RATHO
STREET
DALMAHOY ROAD
LIDGATE SHOT
Ratho
Craigpark
WILKIESTON
LUMSDEN CT
HILLVIEW COTTS
COTTAGES
Pol Sta

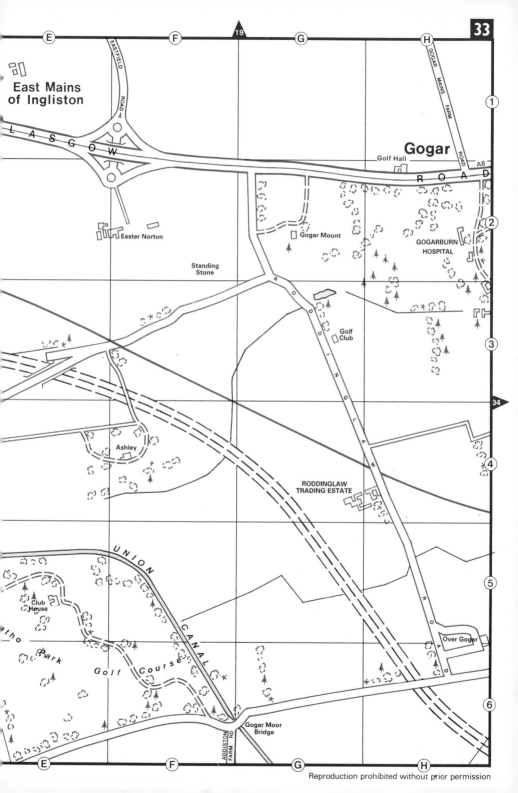

East Mains
of Ingliston

Gogar

GLASGOW

ROAD

Golf Hall

A8

Easter Norton

Gogar Mount

GOGARBURN
HOSPITAL

Standing
Stone

Golf
Club

Ashley

RODDINGLAW
TRADING ESTATE

UNION

CANAL

Club
House

Over Gogar

...tho

Park

Golf   Course

Gogar Moor
Bridge

ADDISTON FARM RD

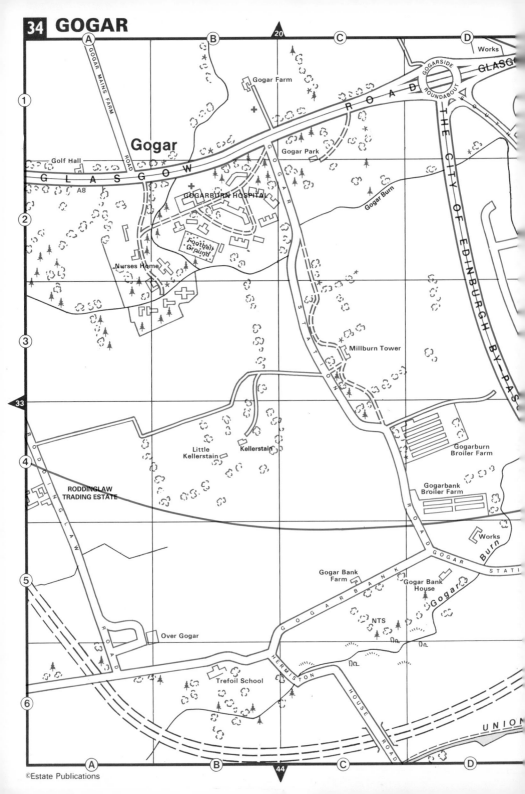

20

A   B   C   D

1

Works

GLASGO

GOGARSIDE ROUNDABOUT

Gogar Farm

GOGAR MAINS FARM

ROAD

Gogar

Gogar Park

Golf Hall

GLASGOW

A8

ROAD

Gogar Burn

GOGARBURN HOSPITAL

2

Football Ground

Nurses Home

STATION

Millburn Tower

3

Gogar Burn

33

ROAD

Little Kellerstain

Kellerstain

Gogarburn Broiler Farm

4

RODDINGLAW TRADING ESTATE

RODDINGLAW

Gogarbank Broiler Farm

ROAD

GOGAR

Works

Burn

STATI

5

Gogar Bank Farm

GOGARBANK

Gogar Bank House

Gogar

Over Gogar

NTS

ROAD

HERMISTON HOUSE ROAD

Trefoil School

6

UNION

©Estate Publications

A   B   C   D

44

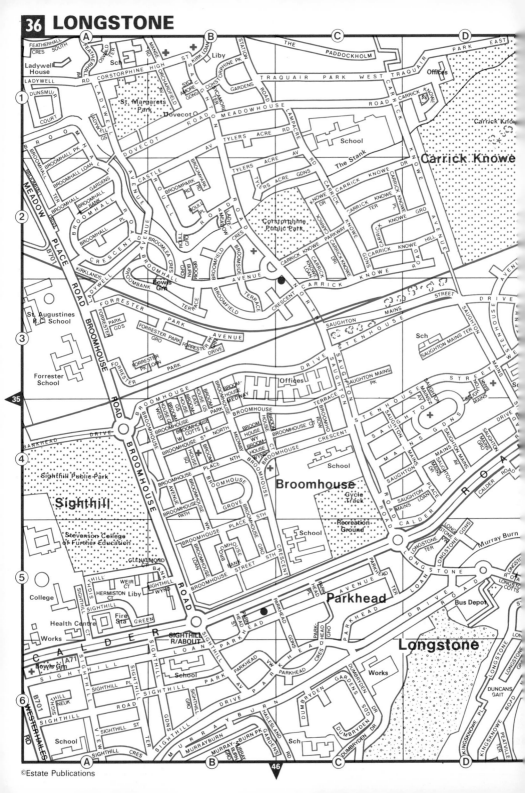

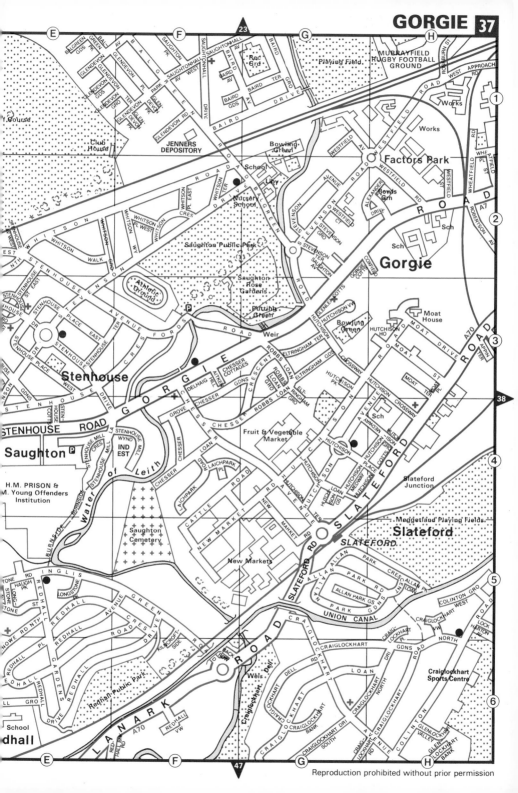

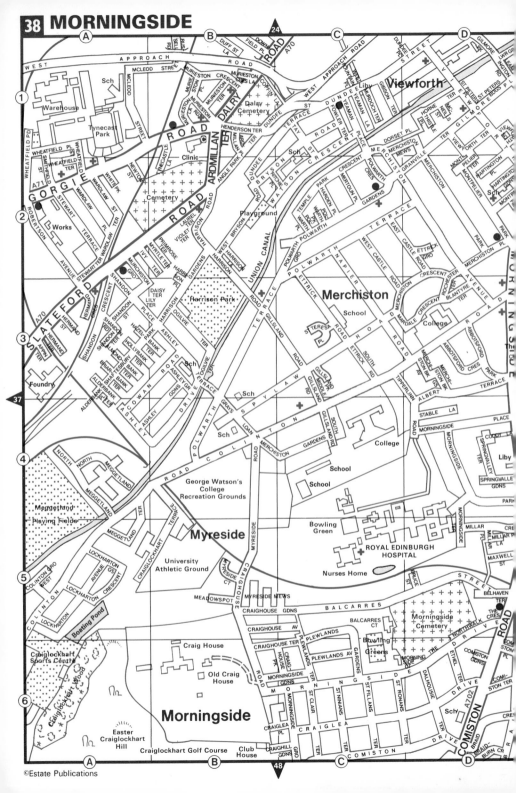

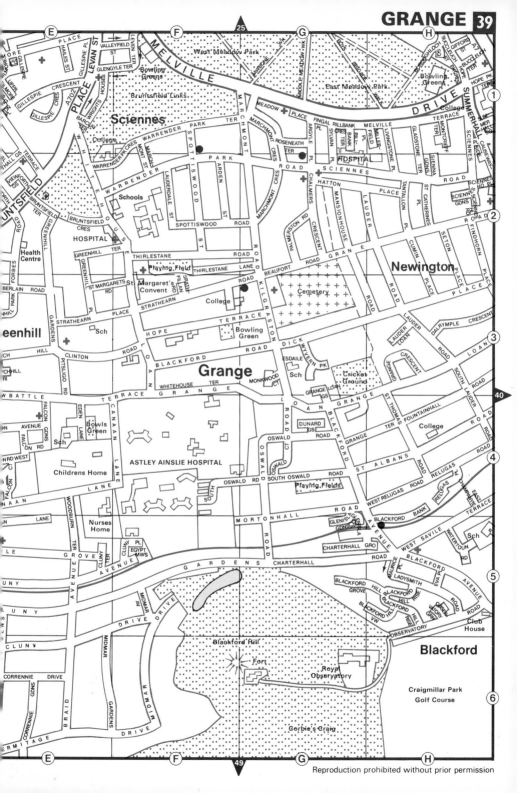

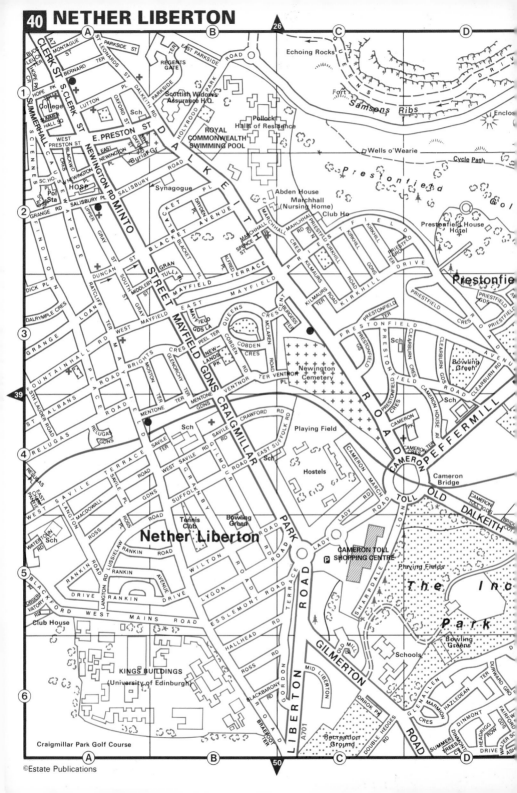

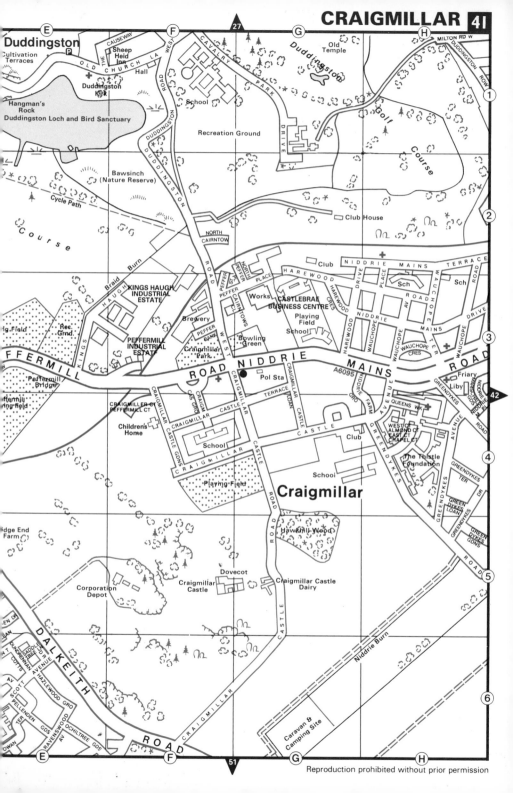

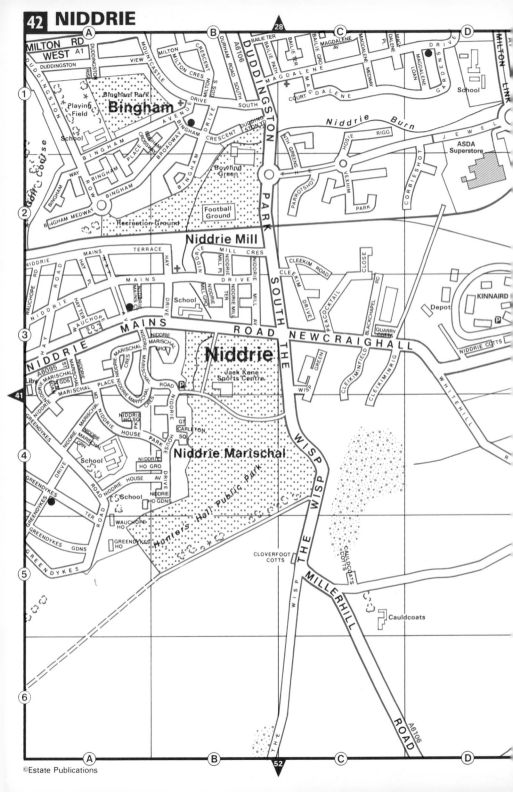

E
Jewel & Esk Valley College
F
29
G
H

Newhailes

1

BRAES
ICHES
INSTANE
RD
GILBERSTOUN PL
SOUTH
STOUN
GILBERSTOUN
Brunstane
Brunstane

ROAD
A6095

Wanton Walls
Bowling Greens
ROAD NEWHAILES
New Hailes Junction

2

Miners Institute

WHITEHILL
NEWCRAIGHALL
ST
Sch
KLONDYKE WAY
PARK TER
NEWCRAIGHALL DR
PARK VIEW
Newcraighall

ROSELBURGH

Newcraighall Public Park

3

ROAD

30

MUCKLETS

4

ROAD
Whitehill Mains

BY-PASS
A1

ITEHILL

5

Millerhill Marshalling Yard

ROAD

Shawfair

FAIR

6

Monktonhall Colliery

E
F
G
H

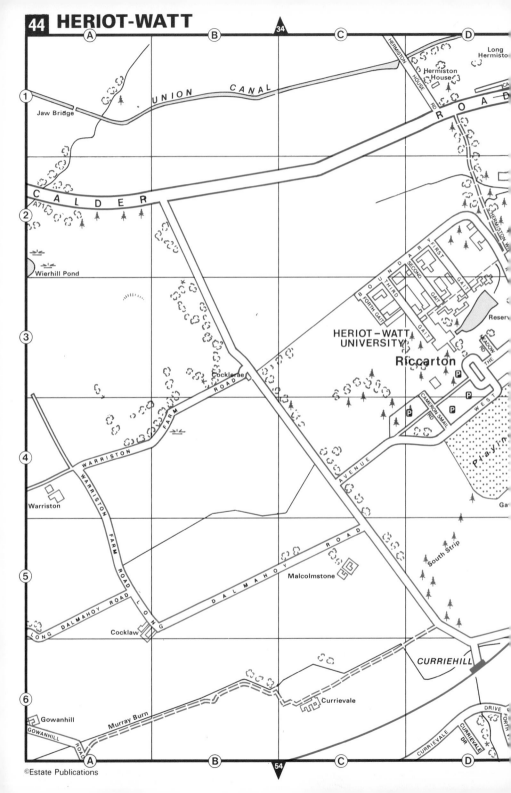

Long Hermiston

UNION CANAL

Jaw Bridge

Hermiston House

CALDER

A71

Wierhill Pond

HERIOT-WATT UNIVERSITY

Riccarton

Cocklerae

FARM ROAD

WARRISTON

Warriston

WARRISTON FARM ROAD

CAMERON SMAIL RD

AVENUE

South Strip

Malcolmstone

DALMAHOY ROAD

LONG

Cocklaw

LONG DALMAHOY ROAD

ROAD

CURRIEHILL

Gowanhill

Murray Burn

Currievale

GOWANHILL ROAD

CURRIEVALE DR

CURRIEVALE

FORTH DRIVE

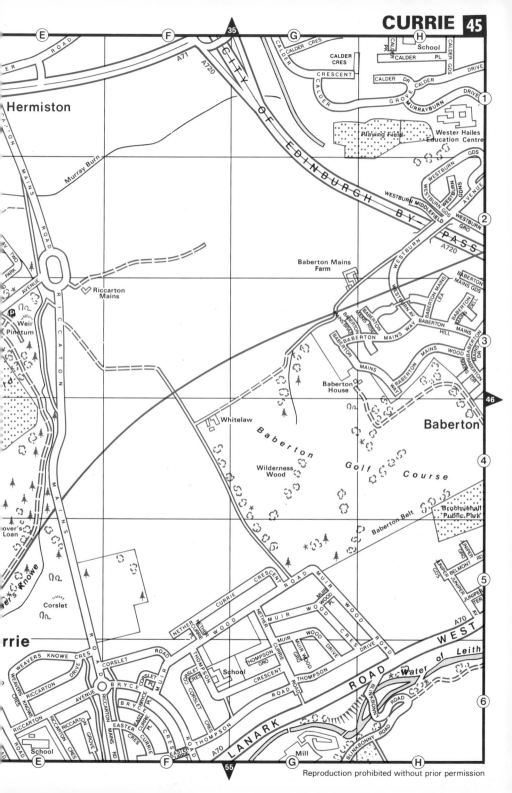

Hermiston

CALDER CRES
CALDER CRES
CALDER PL
CALDER GDS
School
CALDER PK
DRIVE
CALDER DR CALDER
CRESCENT
CALDER
GROVE
MURRAYBURN
DRIVE
1

Murray Burn

Playing Field
Wester Hailes
Education Centre

WESTBURN GDS
GDS
AVENUE
WESTBURN MIDDLEFIELD WESTBURN GRO
WESTBURN
2

CITY OF EDINBURGH BY PASS
A71
A720
A720

Baberton Mains Farm
WESTBURN AV
BABERTON MAINS GDS
BABERTON MAINS DELL
WESTBURN AV
BABERTON MAINS LEA
BABERTON MAINS
Riccarton Mains
BABERTON MAINS WAY
BABERTON MAINS AV
BABERTON MAINS HILL
BABERTON MAINS
3

P
Weir Pinetum
BABERTON MAINS TER
BABERTON MAINS
BABERTON MAINS WOOD
BABERTON MAINS DR
BABERTON MAINS
46

AVENUE
PARK
AV TWO

Whitelaw
Baberton House
Baberton

rd
RICCATON ROAD

B a b e r t o n
G o l f   C o u r s e
4

over's Loan

Wilderness Wood
Broomiehall Public Park
Baberton Belt
5

's Knowe

Corslet
JUNIPER GRO
JUNIPER GDS
BELMONT RD
JUNIPER TER
JUNIPER AV

MAINS ROAD

CRESCENT
CURRIE
ROAD
MUIR WOOD GRO
MUIR WOOD PL
MUIR WOOD CRES
WEST
A70
ROAD of Leith
6

rrie

WEAVERS KNOWE CRES
WEAVERS KNOWE DRIVE
RICCARTON
RICCARTON CRES
CORSLET
BRYCE ROAD
MUIR WOOD ROAD
NETHER CURRIE
NETHER CURRIE
NETHER CRESCENT
MUIR WOOD
THOMPSON CRES
Thompson GRO
CURRIE
MUIR WOOD DRIVE
THOMPSON
ROAD
Water
BLINKBONNY ROAD
ROAD

RICCARTON
AVENUE
RICCARTON GROVE
RICCARTON MAINS RD
BRYCE CRES
BRYCE AV
EASTER CURRIE CRES
CORSLET PL
CORSLET CRES
THOMPSON ROAD
School
Crescent
CURRIE
LANARK
A70
Mill
BLINKBONNY ROAD

School
EASTER CURRIE
E
F
EASTER CURRIE
G
H
55

E   F   G   H

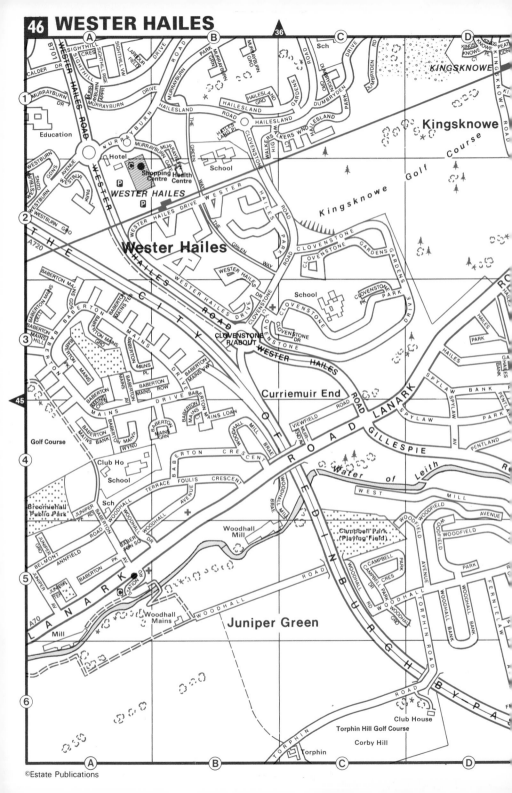

KINGSKNOWE

Kingsknowe

Kingsknowe Golf Course

Wester Hailes

Curriemuir End

Juniper Green

Torphin Hill Golf Course

Corby Hill

Club House

Torphin

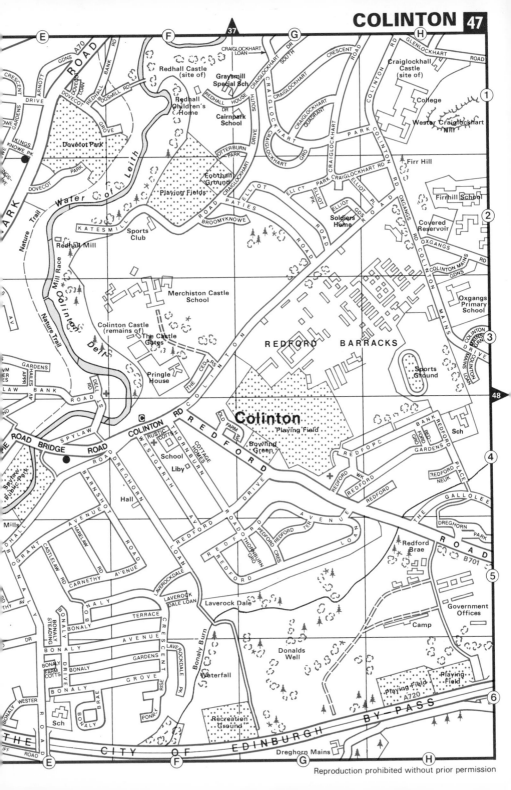

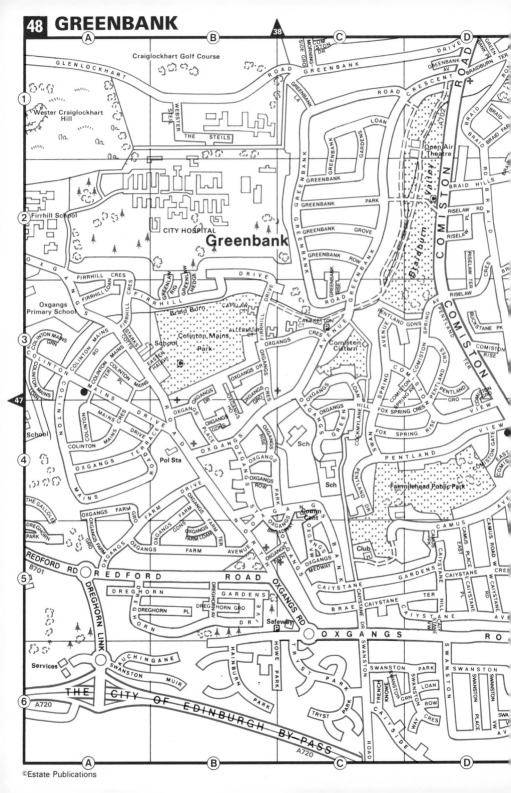

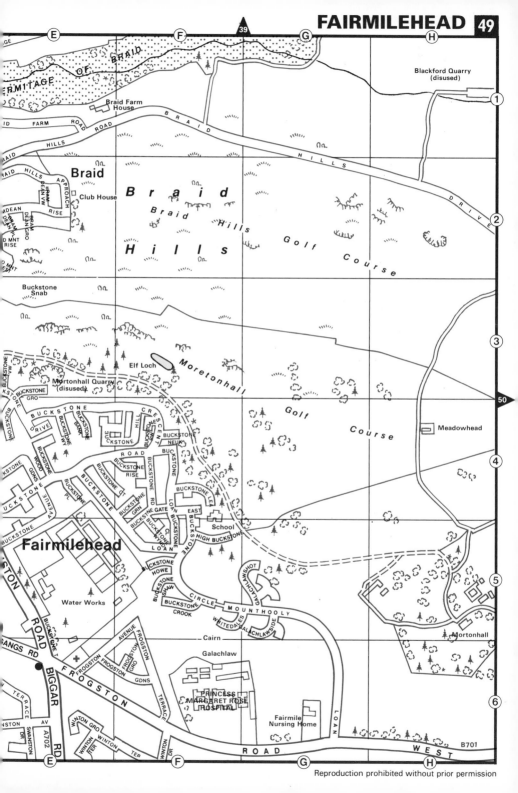

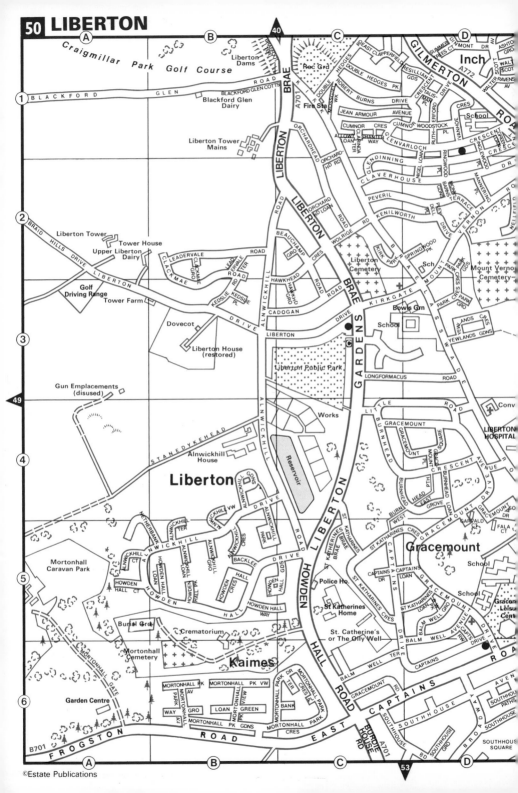

50 LIBERTON

Craigmillar Park Golf Course

Liberton Dams

Rec Grd

Inch A772

EAST CLAPPERFIELD

GILMERTON

SUMMER

CRES

DE MONT

WALTER SCOTT

AV

ASHTON

HESSILIAN GDNS

DOUBLE HEDGES PK

CRESCENT

DRIVE

WALT SCOT

RAVENS

GROVE

DOUBLE HEDGES

ROBERT BURNS DRIVE

WOODSTOCK PL

School

BLACKFORD GLEN COTTS

BLACKFORD GLEN

ROAD

Blackford Glen Dairy

Fire Sta

JEAN ARMOUR AVENUE

RUTH

PL

CRES

JOHNVALE

ROAD

A701

CUMNOR CRES

CUMNO

CRESCENT

Liberton Tower Mains

ORCHARDHEAD

ORCHARD HD RD

CLARINDA TER

SHANTER WAY

GLENVARLOCH

RINGWOOD

INGLEWOOD

RING WOOD

CRES

LIBERTON

ROAD

ORCHARD LOAN

GLENDINNING

CLAVERHOUSE

NIGEL

MANNERING

MOSS

TERRACE

NANTERRE

WELLFIELD

LIBERTON

BRAE

PEVERIL

KENILWORTH

BARNS

PLEY

DELL

VERNON

Liberton Tower

Tower House

Upper Liberton Dairy

LEADERVALE ROAD

BEAUCHAMP GRO

CRES

WOLRIGE RD

ROAD

Mount Vernon Cemetery

BRAID HILLS DRIVE

LIBERTON

CLACKMAE

KEDSLIE RD

KEMP

KEDSLIE PL

HAWKHEAD

HAW HD

HAN HD

Liberton Cemetery

KIRK PARK

B

SPRINGWOOD PK

Sch

SASS

MOUNT VERNON ROAD

CRES

PARK CT PARK

GDNS

GRO

Golf Driving Range

Tower Farm

LEADER VALE RD

ALNWICKHILL

CADOGAN

ROAD

DRIVE

LIBERTON

KIRKGATE

Bowls Grn

School

YEWLANDS CRES

YEWLANDS GDNS

Dovecot

Liberton House (restored)

DRIVE

Liberton Public Park

GARDENS

C

LONGFORMACUS

ROAD

Gun Emplacements (disused)

ALNWICKHILL

LITTLE

ROAD

Conv

Works

BURNHEAD

GRACEMOUNT

LIBERTON HOSPITAL

STANEDYKEHEAD

Alnwickhill House

Reservoir

Liberton

BRAE

GRACEMOUNT

BURNHEAD

MOUNT

BURNHEAD EAST

GROVE

GRACEMOUNT

CRESCENT AVENUE

Mortonhall Caravan Park

ALNWICKHILL GDNS

ALNWICKHILL PARK

BURN

WEST

ST KATHERINES BRAE

GRACEMOUNT DRIVE

CEMOUNT DR

BARDALD

FALA CT

ALNWICKHILL VW

ALNWICKHILL TER

ALNWICKHILL CRES

ST KATHERINES CRES

Gracemount

ALNWICKHILL DRIVE

ALNWICKHILL CRES

ALNWICKHILL PARK

BACKLEE

GDNS

DRIVE

CAPTAINS DR

CAPTAINS LOAN

GRACEMOUNT

School

ALNWICKHILL LOAN

ALNWICKHILL CT

HOWDEN HALL LOAN

HOWDEN HALL CRES

HOWDEN HALL

Police Ho.

ST KATHERINES CRES

School

HOWDEN

HOWDEN HALL CT

HOWDEN HALL GRO

HOWDEN HALL

HOWDEN HALL WAY

St Katherines Home

ST KATHERINES LOAN

BALM WELL GRO

Gracemount Leisure Cent

HOWDEN

Burial Grd

Crematorium

St. Catherine's or The Oily Well

BALM WELL AVENUE

BALM WELL TER

Mortonhall Cemetery

Kaimes

HOWDEN HALL ROAD

GRACEMOUNT RD

CAPTAINS

BALM WELL AVENUE

DRIVE

Garden Centre

MORTONHALL GATE

MORTONHALL PK

MORTONHALL PK VW

MORTONHALL PARK DR

MORTONHALL PARK CRES

MORTONHALL PK GDNS

GRACEMOUNT RD

SOUTHHOUSE

AVEN

SOUTHHOUSE PATHS

MORTONHALL PARK WAY

MORTONHALL PARK AV

MORTONHALL LOAN

MORTONHALL PK GREEN

MORTONHALL PARK BANK

MORTONHALL PARK

CAPTAINS

SOUTHHOUSE

BROADWAY

SOUTHHOUSE SQUARE

B701

FROGSTON

ROAD

EAST

BORDE HOUSE RD

A701

SOUTHHOUSE

SOUTHHOUSE GRO

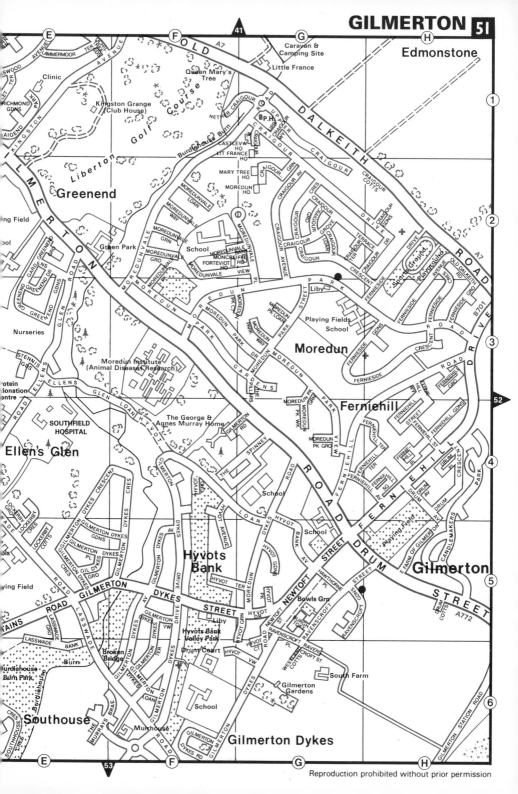

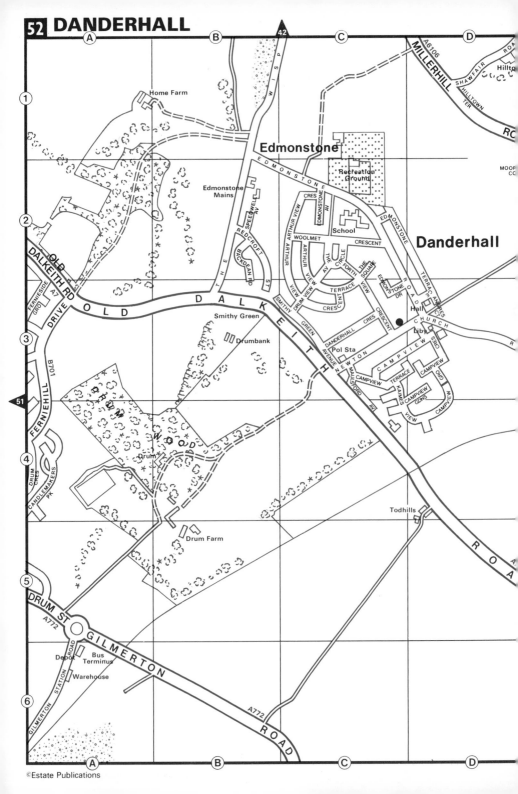

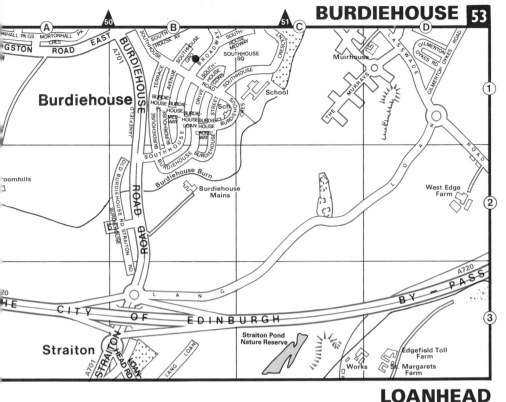

LOANHEAD

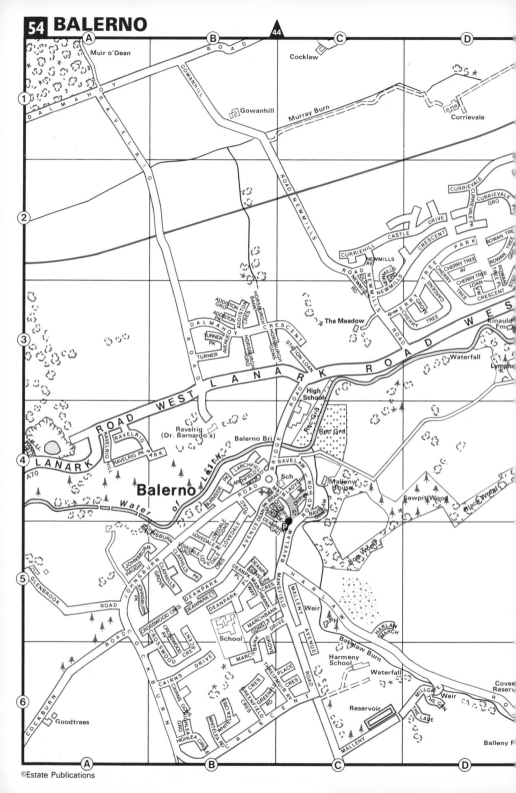

44

A B C D

Muir o'Dean

Cocklaw

① Gowanhill

Murray Burn

Currievale

DALMAHOY

② ROAD NEWMILLS

CURRIEVALE

CURRIEVALE PK

CURRIEVALE GRO

RAVELRIG

CASTLE DRIVE

CURRIEHILL

NEWMILLS AV

PARK

ROWAN TREE

CRESCENT

CHERRY TREE

ROWAN TREE

CHERRY TREE AV

NEWMILLS RD

NEWMILLS

ROWAN TREE PL

③ ADDISTON

ADDISTON GARDENS

ADDISTON PK

HORSBURGH BANK

CHERRY TREE LOAN

CHERRY TREE LW

DALMAHOY

HORSBURGH CRES

HORSBURGH GDNS

CRESCENT

STANTON LOAN

The Meadow

CHERRY GROVE

CHERRY TREE

Kinauld Fm

AVENUE

TURNER PK

HORSBURGH GRO

Waterfall

TURNER

Lymph

ROAD WEST LANARK

ROAD

WEST

LANARK ROAD

RAVELRIG PK

RAVELRIG HILL

RAVELRIG

Ravelrig (Dr. Barnardo's)

RAVELRIG PK

Balerno Bri

High School

Rec Grd

Rec Grd

④ LANARK

A70

Water of Leith

Balerno

LARCHFIELD

LARCHFIELD

BURNSIDE PK

BAVELAW

Sch

MAIN

MALENY ADVERT

MALENY HOUSE

Malleny House

BAVELAW

Sawpit Wood

BRIDGE

ROAD

BRAID

BAVELAW GDNS

Black Wood

DEANPARK GRO

DEANPARK

Bog Wood

⑤ GLENBROOK

JOHNSBURN HAUGH

JOHNSBURN

JOHNSBURN PK

LOVEDALE GDNS

LOVEDALE

LOVEDALE AV

LOVEDALE CRES

CLAYHILLS PK

CLAYHILLS GROVE

AVENUE

BANK

DEANPARK PL

DEANPK

DEANPK PL

MARCHBANK PK

MARCHBANK WAY

MANSFIELD

MALLENY

HARLAW

Weir

Bavelaw Burn

HARLAW MARCH

ROAD

DEANPARK CT

DEANPARK

CROSSWOOD CRES

School

MARCHBANK GDNS

MARCHBANK GROVE

MARCHBANK DRIVE

AVENUE

Harmeny School

CROSSWOOD CRES

CROSSWOOD DRIVE

CAIRNS GDNS

CAIRNS GRO

HIGHLEA GRO

COCKBURN

THREIPMUIR PL

THREIPMUIR AV

GREENFIELD PLACE

GREENFIELD RD

GREENFIELD CRES

MALLENY ROAD

Harmeny School

Waterfall

MILLGATE

THE GLEN

Weir

Cover Reserv

⑥ COCKBURN ROAD

Goodtrees

WHITELEA RD

WHITELEA CRES

HIGHLEA CIRCLE

CRES

Reservoir

THE LADE

MALLENY

Balleny F

A B C D

©Estate Publications

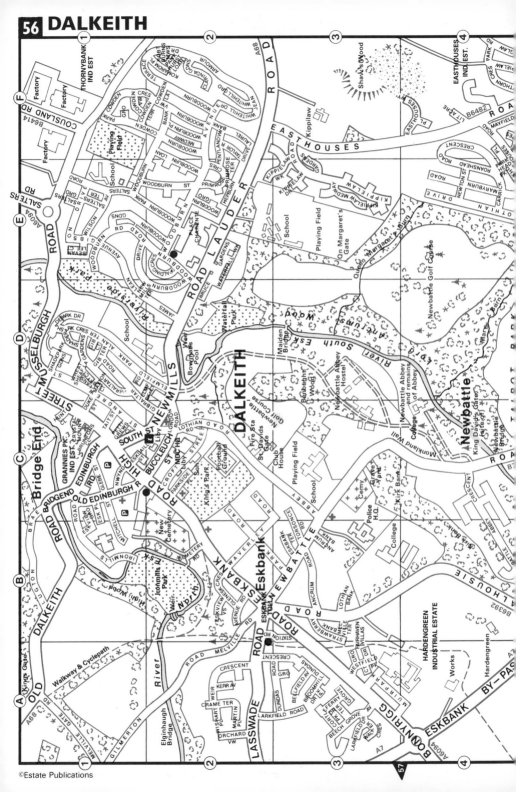

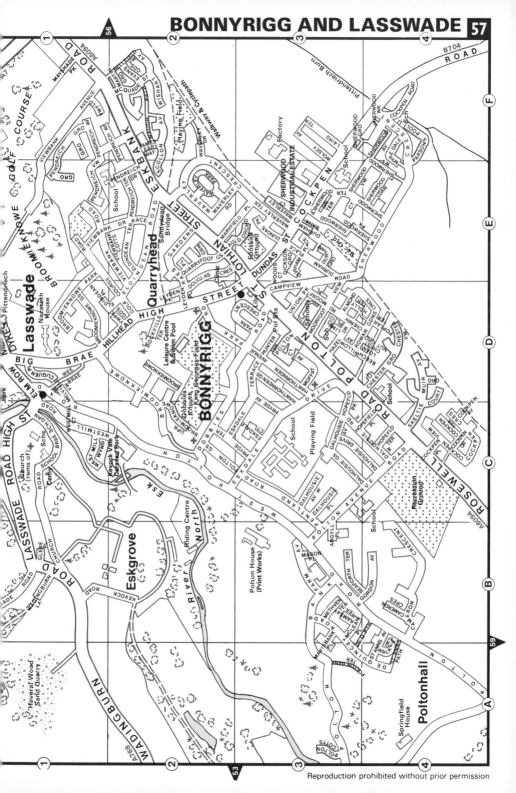

MAYFIELD

NEWTONGRANGE

Easthouses

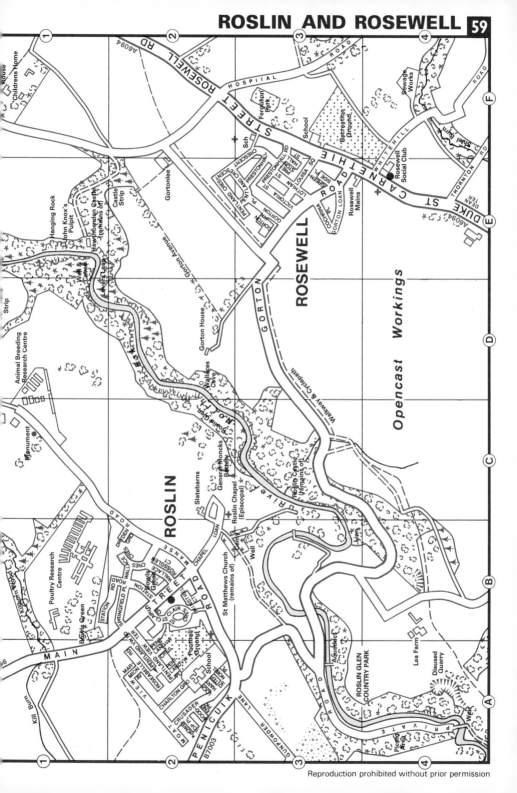

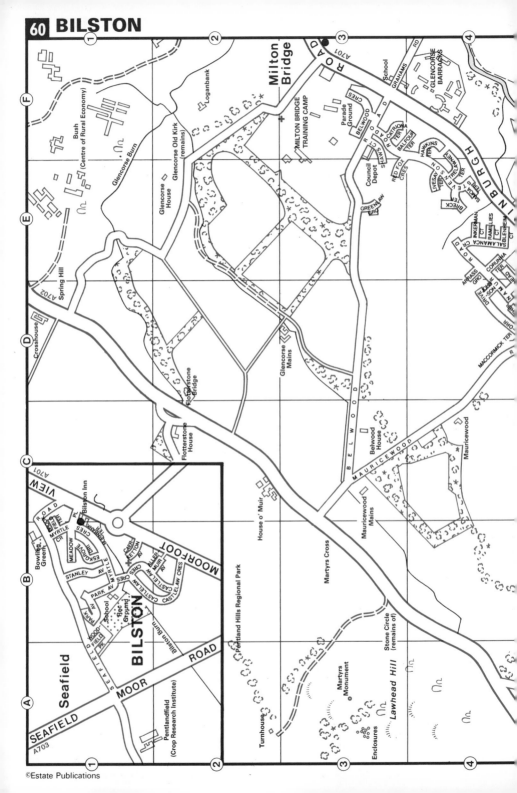

Milton Bridge

Loganbank

Bush (Centre of Rural Economy)

Glencorse Burn

Glencorse House

Glencorse Old Kirk (remains)

MILTON BRIDGE TRAINING CAMP

Parade Ground

School

GRAHAMS

GLENCORSE BARRACKS

BELWOOD

Council Depot

RED FOX CRES

SHAW

CATRIONA

BALFOUR TER

HAWKINS TER

VESEY TER

NELSON STREET

BRECK TER

GREENLAW GRO

INKERMAN CT

SALAMANCA CR

RAMILLIES

BLENHEIM

CORUNNA TER

APRASS GRO

DRIVE

MOSS

CRIMEA

MACCORMICK TER

Spring Hill

A702

Crosshouse

Glencorse Mains

Flotterstone Bridge

Flotterstone House

BELWOOD

MAURICEWOOD

Belwood House

Mauricewood

Mauricewood Mains

VIEW

A701

Bilston Inn

ROAD

BELL TER

MYRTLE CR

MEADOW

ESK GROVE

CAER KETTON

MYRTLE CRES

ALLER

MUIR

PL

PEMBERTON

CRES

MOORFOOT

Bowling Green

STANLEY AV

PARK AV

CASTLELAW AV

CASTLELAW CRES

School

Rec Grpund

FIELD

SEAFIELD DR

PARK AV

WOOD

House o' Muir

Martyrs Cross

Mauricewood Mains

Seafield

BILSTON

MOOR ROAD

Bilston Burn

Pentland Hills Regional Park

SEAFIELD

A703

Pentlandfield (Crop Research Institute)

Turnhouse

Martyrs Monument

Enclosures

Stone Circle (remains of)

Lawhead Hill

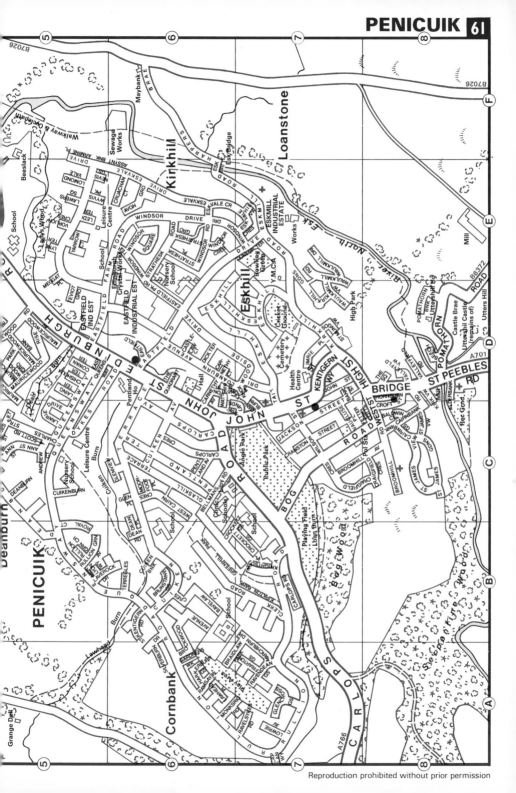

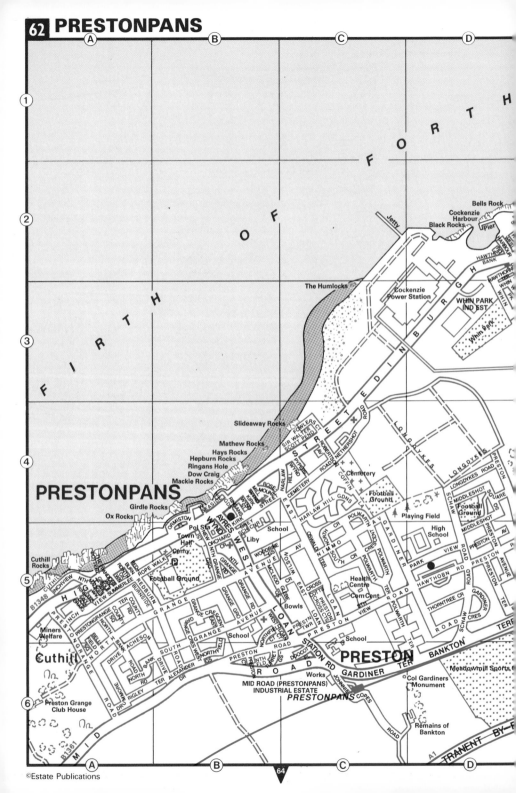

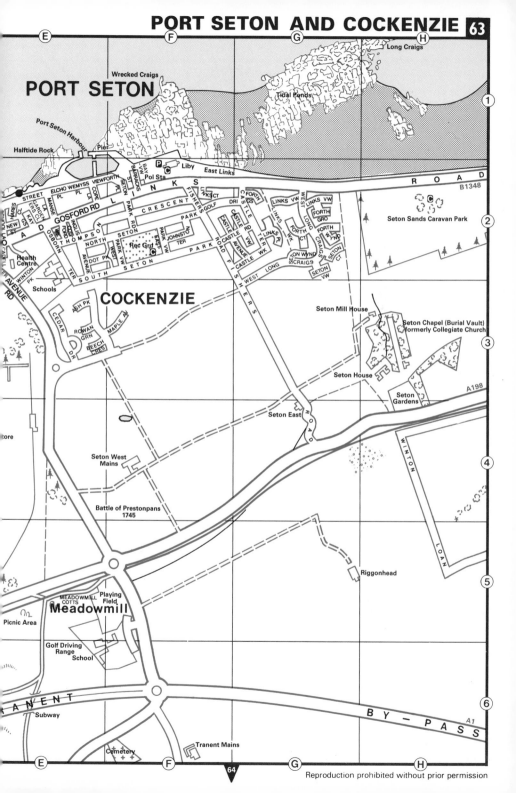

PORT SETON

Long Craigs

Wrecked Craigs

Tidal Ponds

Port Seton Harbour

Halftide Rock Pier

E F G H

1

East Links

Liby Pol Sta

R O A D

B1348

Elcho Wemyss Viewforth

Street

Gosford RD

Crescent

Health Centre

Schools

Seton Sands Caravan Park

2

Rec Grd

COCKENZIE

Ash Pk

Cedar Dr

Rowan Grn

Beech Cres

Maple Av

Seton Mill House

Seton Chapel (Burial Vault)
formerly Collegiate Church

3

Seton House

Seton Gardens

A198

Seton East

Seton West Mains

WINTON LOAN

4

Battle of Prestonpans 1745

Riggonhead

5

Meadowmill Cotts Playing Field

Meadowmill

Picnic Area

Golf Driving Range School

Subway

T R A N E N T

B Y - P A S S A1

6

Tranent Mains

Cemetery

E F G H

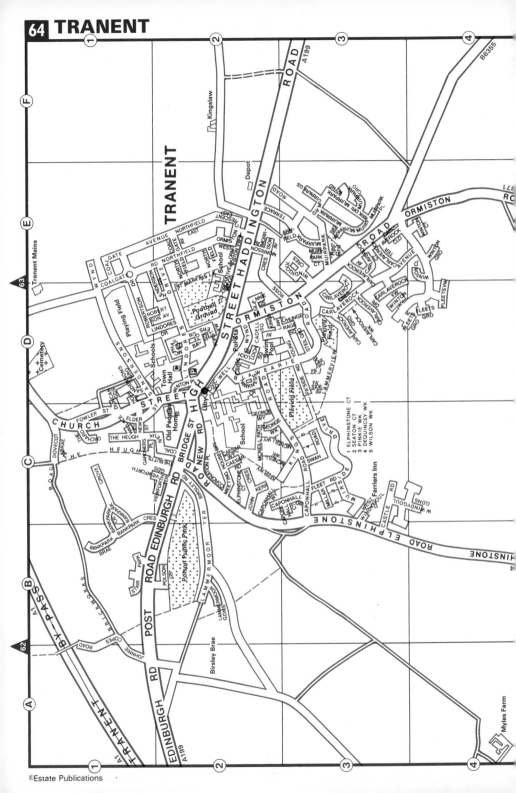

TRANENT

Kingslaw

Depot

Tranent Mains

Cemetery

Playing Field

Football Ground

Schools

Town Hall

Old People's Home

THE HEUGH

Dovecot

Bankpark Park

Birsley Brae

Potsport Public Park

Myles Farm

Farriers Inn

1 ELPHINSTONE CT
2 SEATON CT
3 PINKIE WK
4 DEQUINCEY WK
5 WILSON WK

ORMISTON ROAD

STREET HADDINGTON

HIGH STREET

CHURCH STREET

ROAD EDINBURGH

POST ROAD

ELPHINSTONE ROAD

BY-PASS TRANENT

BRIDGE ST

NEW RD

A199

B6355

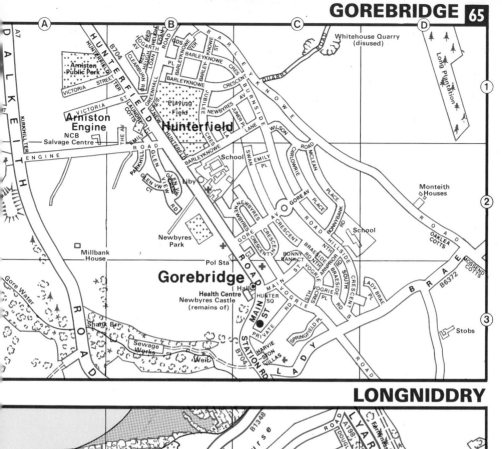

Gorebridge
Hunterfield

LONGNIDDRY

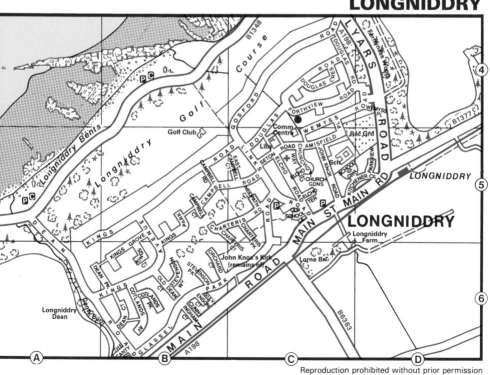

LONGNIDDRY

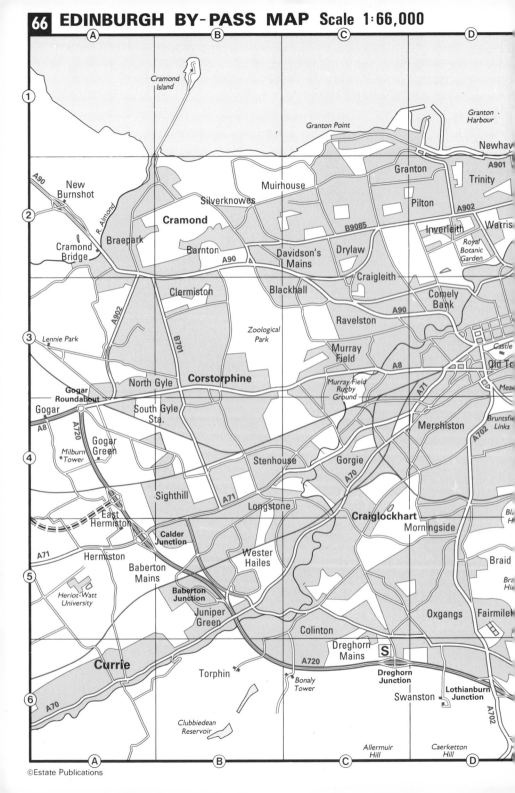

A   B   C   D

1

Cramond
Island

Granton Point

Granton
Harbour

Newhav

A90
New
Burnshot

Muirhouse

Silverknowes

Granton

A901

Trinity

2
Cramond

Barnton

Davidson's
Mains

Pilton

A902

Inverleith

Warris

R. Almond

Braepark

Cramond
Bridge

A90

Drylaw

B9085

Royal
Botanic
Garden

Clermiston

Blackhall

Craigleith

A902

A90

Comely
Bank

3
Lennie Park

B701

Zoological
Park

Ravelston

Murray
Field

Castle

Old Te

North Gyle

Corstorphine

Murray Field
Rugby
Ground

A8

A71

Mea

Gogar
Roundabout

South Gyle
Sta.

Merchiston

A702

Bruntsfi
Links

Gogar
A8

A720

Gogar
Green

A71

Stenhouse

Gorgie

A70

4
Milburn
Tower

Sighthill

A71

Longstone

Craiglockhart

Morningside

Bl
H

East
Hermiston

Calder
Junction

Wester
Hailes

Braid

5
A71

Hermiston

Baberton
Mains

Baberton
Junction

Bra
Hil

Heriot-Watt
University

Juniper
Green

Colinton

Oxgangs

Fairmile

Currie

Torphin

A720

Dreghorn
Mains

S

Dreghorn
Junction

6
A70

Bonaly
Tower

Swanston

Lothianburn
Junction

A702

Clubbiedean
Reservoir

Allermuir
Hill

Caerketton
Hill

A   B   C   D

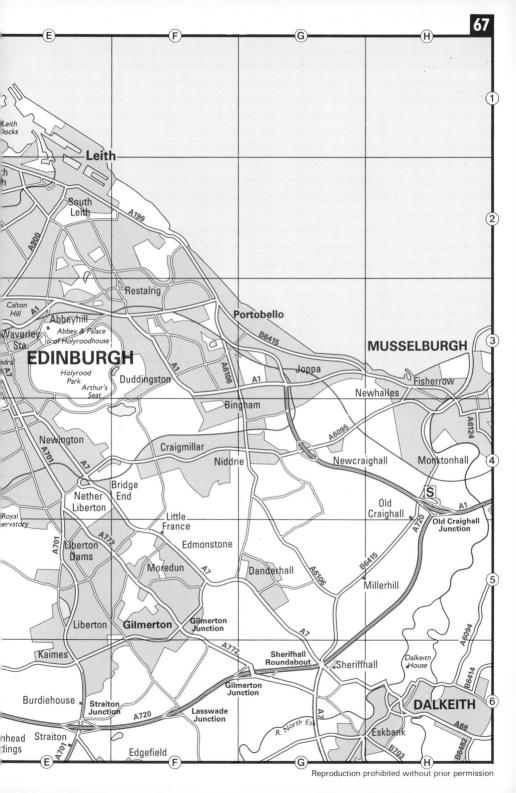

E F G H

1
2
3
4
5
6

Leith Docks

Leith

South Leith

A199

A900

Restalrig

Calton Hill

A1

Abbeyhill

Waverley Sta.

Abbey & Palace of Holyroodhouse

Portobello

B6415

MUSSELBURGH

EDINBURGH

Holyrood Park

Arthur's Seat

Duddingston

A1

A6106

A1

Joppa

Fisherrow

Newhailes

Bingham

Newington

A701

A7

Craigmillar

Niddrie

A6095

Newcraighall

A6124

Monktonhall

Royal Observatory

Nether Liberton

Bridge End

Little France

Old Craighall

S

A1

A720

Old Craighall Junction

Liberton Dams

A701

A172

Edmonstone

Danderhall

A6106

B6415

Millerhill

Moredun

A7

Liberton

Gilmerton

Gilmerton Junction

A7

A6094

Kaimes

A772

Sheriffhall Roundabout

Sheriffhall

Dalkeith House

B6414

Burdiehouse

Straiton Junction

A720

Gilmerton Junction

Lasswade Junction

A7

DALKEITH

A68

nhead dings

Straiton

A701

Edgefield

R. North Esk

Eskbank

B703

B6482

A68

INDEX TO STREETS

EDINBURGH GLOSSARY

CLOSE - Gated entrance to Tenement with access to rear of building
COURT - A courtyard
LAND - A Tenement
PEND - An archway
VENNEL - Passage or Lane
WYND - An open thoroughfare

The Index includes some names for which there is insufficient space on the maps. These names are preceded by an * and are followed by the nearest adjoining thoroughfare.

Abbey Hill	26 B3
Abbey La	26 C3
Abbey Strand	5 H2
Abbey St	26 B2
Abbeyhill	5 H2
Abbeyhill Cres	5 H2
Abbeymount	5 H1
Abbotsford Cres	38 D3
Abbotsford Park	38 D3
Abercorn Cotts	27 F6
Abercorn Ct	27 G5
Abercorn Cres	27 F4
Abercorn Dri	27 F4
Abercorn Gdns	27 G3
Abercorn Gro	27 F4
Abercorn Pl	27 F4
Abercorn Rd	27 F4
Abercorn Ter	28 D4
Abercromby Pl	4 C1
Abinger Gdns	23 H5
Academy St	16 B5
Addiston Farm Rd	33 F6
Addiston Gro	54 B3
Addiston Park	54 B3
Adelphi Gro	28 B3
Adelphi Pl	28 B4
Admiral Ter	39 E2
Admiralty St	15 A3
Advocates Clo	4 D3
Afton Pl	14 D4
Afton Ter	14 D3
Agnew Ter	15 G4
Ainslie Pl	24 D3
Aitchs Pl	28 C3
Aitken Hill	37 F3
Alan Breck Gdns	22 A3
Albany La	25 G2
Albany St	25 G2
Albany St Lane	25 G2
Albert Pl	26 A1
Albert Rd	16 D3
Albert St	26 A1
Albert Ter	38 D3
Albion Pl	26 C1
Albion Rd	26 B1
Albion Ter	26 C1
Albyn Pl	4 A2
Alderbank Pl	38 A3
Alderbank Ter	38 A3
Alexander Dri	37 H2
Alfred Pl	40 B2
Allan Park	8 D2
Allan Park Cres	37 G5
Allan Park Gdns	37 G5
Allan Park Loan	37 H5
Allan Park Rd	37 G5
Allan St	24 D2
Allanfield	26 B1
Allermuir Ct	48 B3
Allermuir Rd	47 E5
Allison Pl	8 D2
Alloway Loan	50 C1
Almond Av	19 E5
Almond Bank Cotts	11 G3
Almond Bank Ter	38 A3
Almond Ct, Braepark	11 E6
Almond Ct, Craigmillar	41 H4
Almond Grn	21 E4
Almond Rd	18 D5
Almond Sq	21 F4
Almondhill Rd	8 D2

Almondside	8 E2
Alnwickhill Ct	50 A5
Alnwickhill Cres	50 B5
Alnwickhill Dri	50 B5
Alnwickhill Gdns	50 B4
Alnwickhill Gro	50 B5
Alnwickhill Loan	50 B5
Alnwickhill Park	50 B4
Alnwickhill Rd	50 B3
Alnwickhill Ter	50 B5
Alnwickhill View	50 B5
Alva Pl	26 B2
Alva St	24 D4
Anchor Clo	5 E3
Anchorfield	15 H2
Anderson Pl	16 A4
Andrew Wood Ct	15 F2
Angle Park Ter	38 B2
Angres Ct	52 D3
Ann St	24 D2
Annandale St	25 H1
Annandale St Lane	25 H1
Annfield, Newhaven	15 G2
Annfield, Wester Hailes	46 A5
Annfield St	15 G2
Appin Ter	38 A3
Arboretum Av	24 D1
Arboretum Pl	14 D6
Arboretum Rd	14 D5
Archibald Pl	4 C6
Arden St	39 F2
Ardmillan Pl	38 B1
Ardmillan Ter	38 B2
Ardsheil Av	22 A3
Argyle Cres	28 D4
Argyle Pl	39 G1
Argyle St	16 A3
Argyll Ter	24 D6
Arnott Gdns	47 E1
Arran Pl	28 D4
Arthur St	16 A6
Arthur St Lane	16 A6
Arthur View Cres	52 C2
Arthur View Ter	52 C2
Ashley Dri	38 A4
Ashley Gdns	38 B4
Ashley Grn	38 B3
Ashley Pl	15 H5
Ashley Ter	38 B3
Ashton Gro	40 D6
Ashton Villas	28 D5
Ashville Ter	16 C6
Assembly St	16 C3
Atholl Cres	24 D5
Atholl Cres La	24 D5
Atholl Ter	24 D6
Auchingane	48 A6
Auchinleck Ct	15 G2
Auldgate	8 E2
Avenue Views	24 B2
Avenue West	44 C4
Avon Ct	11 F4
Avon Gro	11 F5
Avon Pl	11 F5
Avon Rd	11 E5
Avondale Pl	25 E1

Baberton Cres	46 B4
Baberton Mains Av	46 A3
Baberton Mains Bank	46 A4
Baberton Mains Brae	45 G3
Baberton Mains Ct	46 B4
Baberton Mains Cres	46 A3
Baberton Mains Dell	46 A3
Baberton Mains Dri	46 A3
Baberton Mains Gdns	46 A3
Baberton Mains Grn	46 B4
Baberton Mains Gro	46 A3
Baberton Mains Hill	45 H4
Baberton Mains Lea	45 H3
Baberton Mains Loan	46 B3
Baberton Mains Park	46 A3
Baberton Mains Pl	46 A3
Baberton Mains Rise	45 H3
Baberton Mains Row	46 A3
Baberton Mains Ter	46 A3
Baberton Mains Vw	46 B3
Baberton Mains Way	45 H3
Baberton Mains Wood	45 H3
Baberton Mains Wynd	46 A4
Baberton Park	46 A5

Baberton Sq	46 A5
Back Dean	24 B3
Back Row	37 F6
*Back Station Rd, North Peffer Pl	41 G2
Back Walk	26 B3
Backdean Rd	52 B2
Backlee	50 B5
Baileyfield Cres	28 B4
Baileyfield Rd	28 A3
Baileyfield Rd	28 B4
Bailie Fifes Clo	5 E3
Bailie Path	42 B1
Bailie Pl	28 C6
Bailie Ter	28 B6
Baird Av	37 F1
Baird Dri	37 F1
Baird Gdns	37 F1
Baird Gro	37 G1
Baird Rd	32 B4
Baird Ter	37 G1
Bake House Clo	5 G3
Balbirnie Pl	24 A5
Balcarres Ct	38 C5
Balcarres St	38 C5
Balderston Gdns	50 D1
Balfour Pl	16 A5
Balfour St	16 A5
Balfron Loan	21 H3
Balgreen Av	23 E6
Balgreen Gdns	23 E6
Balgreen Park	23 E6
Balgreen Rd	37 F1
Ballantyne La	16 A4
Ballantyne Rd	16 A4
Balm Well Av	50 D6
Balm Well Gro	50 D5
Balm Well Park	50 D5
Balm Well Ter	50 C6
Balmoral Pl	25 E1
Baltic St	16 C3
Bangholm Av	15 E4
Bangholm Bower Av	15 E4
Bangholm Gro	15 F4
Bangholm Loan	15 F4
Bangholm Park	15 E4
Bangholm Pl	15 E4
Bangholm Rd	15 E4
Bangholm Ter	15 E5
Bangholm View	15 F4
Bangor Rd	16 A4
Bank St	4 D3
Bankhead Av	35 H4
Bankhead Broadway	35 G4
Bankhead Crossway Nth	35 G5
Bankhead Crossway Sth	35 G5
Bankhead Dri	35 F4
Bankhead Loan	35 H5
Bankhead Medway	35 G5
Bankhead St	35 H4
Bankhead Ter	35 G5
Bankhead Way	35 G5
Barclay Ter	39 E1
Barnshot Rd	47 E4
Barnton Av	12 A6
Barnton Av West	11 H5
Barnton Brae	11 G5
Barnton Ct	21 G1
Barnton Gdns	12 B4
Barnton Gro	21 F1
Barnton Loan	12 B5
Barnton Park	12 B5
Barnton Park Av	21 H1
Barnton Park Cres	21 G1
Barnton Park Dell	22 A1
Barnton Park Dri	21 H1
Barnton Park Gdns	21 G1
Barnton Park Gro	11 H6
Barnton Park Pl	22 A1
Barnton Park View	21 G1
Barnton Park Wood	21 G1
Barnton Ter	24 A2
Baronscourt Rd	27 F3
Baronscourt Ter	27 F3
Barony Pl	25 G2
Barony St	25 G2
Barrace Steps	4 B4
Bartongate Av	21 F2
Bartongate Dri	21 G2
Bartongate Ter	21 G1
Bath Pl	28 C3

Bath Rd	16 D3
Bath St	28 C4
Bath St Lane	28 C4
Bathfield	15 H2
Bavelaw Gdns	54 C4
Bavelaw Rd	54 C4
Beach La	28 C3
Beachfield	15 G5
Beauchamp Gro	50 C2
Beauchamp Rd	50 C2
Beaufort Rd	39 G2
Beaverbank Pl	15 G6
Beaverhall Rd	15 G6
Bedford St	24 D2
Bedford Ter	28 D4
Beechmount Cres	23 F6
Beechmount Mains	23 E6
Beechwood Ter	16 D6
Belford Av	24 A3
Belford Bri	24 C4
Belford Gdns	24 A3
Belford Mews	24 C4
Belford Park	24 B4
Belford Pl	24 B4
Belford Rd	24 C4
Belford Ter	24 C4
Belgrave Cres	24 C3
Belgrave Cres La	24 C3
Belgrave Gdns	22 C6
Belgrave Mews	24 C3
Belgrave Pl	22 B6
Belgrave Rd	22 B6
Belgrave Ter	22 B6
Belhaven Ter	38 D5
Bell La	25 G1
Bell Pl	25 E1
Bellenden Gdns	41 E6
Bellevue	25 G1
Bellevue Cres	25 G1
Bellevue Gdns	25 G1
Bellevue Gro	25 H1
Bellevue Pl	25 G1
Bellevue Rd	25 G1
Bellevue St	25 G1
Bellevue Ter	25 G1
Bellfield La	28 C4
Bellfield St	28 C4
Bellfield Ter	28 C4
Bells Brae	24 D3
Bells Wynd	5 E3
Belmont Av	23 F5
Belmont Cres	23 F5
Belmont Gdns	23 F5
Belmont Park	23 F5
Belmont Rd	46 A5
Belmont Ter	23 F5
Belmont Vw	23 F5
Beresford Av	15 F3
Beresford Gdns	15 F3
Beresford Pl	15 E3
Beresford Ter	15 E3
Bernard St	16 C3
Bernard Ter	40 A1
Biggar Rd	49 E6
Bingham Av	42 A1
Bingham Broadway	42 A2
Bingham Cres	42 B1
Bingham Crossway	42 B1
Bingham Dri	42 B2
Bingham Medway	42 A2
Bingham Pl	42 A2
Bingham Way	42 A2
Birch Ct	21 F2
Birnies Ct	13 E4
Bishops Clo	5 E3
Blackbarony Rd	40 B6
Blackchapel Rd	42 C3
Blacket Av	40 B2
Blacket Pl	40 B2
Blackford Av	39 G4
Blackford Bank	39 H5
Blackford Glen Cotts	50 B1
Blackford Glen Rd	50 A1
Blackford Hill Gro	39 G5
Blackford Hill Rise	39 H5
Blackford Hill View	39 H5
Blackford Rd	39 F3
Blackfriars St	5 E3
Blackie Rd	16 D5
Blackthorn Ct	21 F2
Blackwood Cres	40 A2
Blaeberry Gdns	21 F2
Blair St	5 E4

Blantyre Ter	38 D4
Blenheim Pl	5 H1
Blinkbonny Av	23 H4
Blinkbonny Cres	23 G4
Blinkbonny Gdns	23 H4
Blinkbonny Gro	23 H4
Blinkbonny Gro West	23 H4
Blinkbonny Rd, Currie	54 C1
Blinkbonny Rd, Ravelston	23 H4
Blinkbonny Ter	23 G4
Boat Grn	25 F1
Bogsmill Rd	37 H4
Bonaly Av	47 E4
Bonaly Brae	47 E5
Bonaly Cres	47 E5
Bonaly Dri	46 D4
Bonaly Farm Cotts	47 F6
Bonaly Gdns	47 E5
Bonaly Gro	47 E5
Bonaly Rise	47 F5
Bonaly Road	46 D4
Bonaly Steading	46 D5
Bonaly Ter	47 E5
Bonaly Wester	46 D5
Bonar Pl	15 H4
Bonnington Av	15 H4
Bonnington Gro	15 H4
Bonnington Rd	16 A4
Bonnington Ter	15 H4
Bonnyhaugh	15 H4
Bonnyhaugh La	15 H4
Boothacre Cotts	17 G6
Boothacre La	17 F6
Borthwalk Pl	41 G1
Borthwick Clo	5 E3
Boswall Av	14 D4
Boswall Cres	14 D4
Boswall Dri	14 D4
Boswall Gdns	14 D4
Boswall Grn	15 E4
Boswall Gro	14 D4
Boswall Loan	14 D4
Boswall Medway	14 D4
Boswall Parkway	14 C4
Boswall Pl	14 D4
Boswall Quadrant	14 D4
Boswall Rd	15 E3
Boswall Sq	14 D4
Boswall Ter	14 D4
Boswells Ct	5 E3
Bothwell St	26 B1
Boundary Rd	20 A2
Bowhill Ter	15 E5
Bowling Green Clo	5 G3
Bowling Green Rd	9 H1
Bowmont Pl	40 A1
Boyds Entry	5 E4
Boys Brigade Walk	39 H1
Brae Park	11 F6
Brae Park Rd	11 F6
Braefoot Ter	41 F5
Braehead Av	11 F6
Braehead Bank	11 F6
Braehead Cres	11 F6
Braehead Dri	11 F6
Braehead Gro	11 F6
Braehead Loan	11 F6
Braehead Mews	11 F6
Braehead Park	11 F6
Braehead Rd	11 E6
Braehead Row	11 F6
Braehead Vw	11 F6
Braid Av	39 F4
Braid Cres	39 E4
Braid Farm Rd	39 F5
Braid Hills App	48 D2
Braid Hills Av	39 E5
Braid Hills Cres	39 E5
Braid Hills Dri	39 G5
Braid Hills Rd	39 E6
Braid Mount	39 F6
Braid Mount Cres	39 F6
Braid Mount Rise	39 F6
Braid Mount View	39 F6
Braid Rd	39 E4
Braidburn Cres	38 D5
Braidburn Ter	38 D5
Bramble Dri	21 F2
Bramdean Gro	39 E6
Bramdean Pl	39 E6
Bramdean Rise	39 E6
Bramdean View	39 E6

68

Dri 28 C6
Gdns 28 D6
Pl 26 C2
field St 24 D6
on St 25 F1
on Ter 25 F1
St 4 A5
St Ct 4 A5
Ter 24 D6
bane St 16 A4
ank Ter 38 A3
eld 28 B3
Pl 24 D1
Rd, Balerno 54 B4
Rd, Colinton 47 E4
St, Newbridge 9 C6
St, Portobello 28 B3
St La 28 B3
nd Cotts 40 D5
Bauks 5 F5
Ter 24 D6
on Pl 28 B4
on St 5 E5
s Cres 40 A3
Pl 4 D5
Port 4 D5
Sq 5 E5
ll Cres 27 G2
Wynd 16 B3
s Clo 4 D4
bank Ter 36 A2
burn Gro 36 B2
field Cres 36 B2
hall Av 36 B2
hall Bank 36 A2
hall Cres 36 A2
hall Dri 35 H1
hall Gdns 36 A2
hall Loan 36 A2
hall Park 36 A2
hall Pl 36 A2
hall Rd 36 A1
hall Ter 36 A1
house Av 36 B4
house Bank 36 B5
house Cotts East 36 B4
house Cotts West 36 B4
house Ct 36 B4
house Cres 36 B4
house Dri 36 A4
house Gdns 36 B4
house Gdns East 36 B3
house Gdns West 36 B4
house Gro 36 B4
house Loan 36 B5
house Medway 36 B3
house Park 36 B4
house Path 36 B4
house Pl Nth 36 B4
house Pl Sth 36 B5
house Rd 36 A3
house Row 36 C4
house Sq 36 B4
house St Nth 36 B4
house St Sth 36 B5
house Ter 36 B4
house Walk 36 B4
house Way 36 B4
house Wynd 36 B4
lea Cres 36 B2
park Rd 36 B2
side Ter 36 B2
yknowe 47 F2
ham Pl 4 B6
ham St 4 B6
nton Market 25 G2
nton Pl 25 H2
nton Pl Lane 25 H2
nton Rd 15 G6
nton St 25 G2
nton St La 25 H2
St 5 F5
St La 5 F5
s Clo 5 G2
s Ct 5 G3
s Pl 4 C5
St 38 D5
ane Bank 29 E6
ane Cres 29 F6
ane Dri 29 E6
ane Gdns 28 D5
ane Gdns Mews 28 D5
ane Rd 28 D5
ane Rd Nth 28 D4
ane Rd Sth 28 D6
wick Pl 26 A1
wick Rd 26 A1
wick St 26 A1
wick St Lane 26 A2
wick Ter 26 B1

Brunton Pl 26 B2
Brunton Ter 26 B2
Bruntsfield Av 38 D2
Bruntsfield Cres 39 E2
Bruntsfield Gdns 39 E2
Bruntsfield Pl 39 E2
Bruntsfield Ter 39 E2
Bryce Av 27 H2
Bryce Cres 55 F1
Bryce Gro 27 H2
Bryce Rd 55 F1
Bryson Rd 38 B2
Buccleuch Pl 5 E6
Buccleuch Pl Lane 25 H6
Buccleuch St 5 E6
Buccleuch Ter 39 H1
Buchanan St 16 B6
Buckingham Ter 24 C3
Buckstane Park 48 D3
Buckstone Av 49 E5
Buckstone Bank 49 E4
Buckstone Circle 49 F5
Buckstone Clo 49 F5
Buckstone Ct 49 E4
Buckstone Cres 49 E4
Buckstone Crook 49 F5
Buckstone Dell 49 E4
Buckstone Dri 49 E3
Buckstone Gdns 49 E4
Buckstone Gate 49 F5
Buckstone Grn 49 F4
Buckstone Gro 49 E3
Buckstone Hill 49 F4
Buckstone Howe 49 F5
Buckstone Lea 49 F4
Buckstone Loan 49 E4
Buckstone Loan East 49 F4
Buckstone Neuk 49 F4
Buckstone Pl 49 E4
Buckstone Rise 49 F4
Buckstone Road 49 F4
Buckstone Row 49 F4
Buckstone Shaw 49 F5
Buckstone Ter 48 D4
Buckstone View 49 E3
Buckstone Way 49 E4
Buckstone Wood 49 E4
Buckstone Wynd 49 F5
Bughtlin Gdns 21 F3
Bughtlin Grn 21 F3
Bughtlin Loan 21 F3
Bughtlin Pl 21 F3
Bughtlin Rd 21 F3
Bulls Clo 5 G3
Burdiehouse Av 53 B1
Burdiehouse Cres 53 B1
Burdiehouse Crossway 53 B1
Burdiehouse Dri 53 B2
Burdiehouse Loan 53 B1
Burdiehouse Medway 53 B1
Burdiehouse Pl 53 B1
Burdiehouse Rd 53 B1
Burdiehouse Sq 53 B2
Burdiehouse St 53 B2
Burdiehouse Ter 53 B1
Burgess St 16 B3
Burgess Ter 40 C3
Burgh Toft 51 G5
Burlington St 16 A4
Burnbrae 21 F4
Burnets Clo 5 E3
Burnhead Cres 50 C4
Burnhead Gro 50 C4
Burnhead Loan 50 D4
Burnhead Path East 50 D4
Burnhead Path West 50 C4
Burns St 16 C5
Burnside, Bughtlin 21 F4
Burnside, Saughton 37 E4
Burnside Park 54 B4
Buroughloch Sq 39 H1
Byers Clo 4 D3

Cables Wynd 16 B4
Cables Wynd Ho 16 B4
Caddells 11 G3
Cadiz St 16 C3
Cadogan Rd 50 B3
Cadzow Pl 26 C2
Caerketton Ct 48 C3
*Cairngor Ho,
Lindsay Rd 16 A2
Cairnmuir Rd 22 B5
Cairns Dri 54 B6
Cairns Gdns 54 B6
Cairntows Clo 41 F3
Caiyside 48 C6
Caiystane Av 48 D5
Caiystane Cres 48 D5
Caiystane Dri 48 C5
Caiystane Gdns 48 C5
Caiystane Hill 48 D5
Caiystane Ter 48 C6
Caiystane View 48 D5
Calder Ct 35 H6
Calder Cres 45 G1
Calder Dri 45 H1
Calder Gdns 35 G6
Calder Gro 45 G1
Calder Park 35 H6
Calder Pl 45 H1
Calder Rd, Hermiston 44 A2
Calder Rd, Longstone 36 A6
Calder Rd Gdns 36 D4
Calder Vier 35 G6
Caledonian Cres 24 C6
Caledonian Pl 4 C6
Caledonian Rd 24 C6
Calton Hill 5 E2
Calton Hill Stairs 5 F2
Calton Rd 5 E2
Cambridge Av 16 A6
Cambridge Gdns 16 A6
Cambridge St 4 A4
Cambridge St Lane 4 A4
Cambusnethan St 26 D2
Cameron Cres 40 D4
Cameron House Av 40 D4
Cameron March 40 C4
Cameron Park 40 C4
Cameron Smail Rd 44 D4
Cameron Ter 40 D4
Cameron Toll 40 C4
Cameron Toll Gdns 40 D4
Cammo Bank 21 F1
Cammo Brae 21 E1
Cammo Gdns 21 E1
Cammo Gro 21 E1
Cammo Hill 21 E1
Cammo Parkway 21 E1
Cammo Pl 21 E1
Cammo Rd 19 H2
Cammo Walk 21 E2
Campbell Av 23 G5
Campbell Park Cres 46 C5
Campbell Park Dri 46 C5
Campbell Rd 23 G4
Campbells Clo 5 G2
Campview 52 C3
Campview Cres 52 D3
Campview Gdns 52 D3
Campview Gro 52 D4
Campview Ter 52 C3
Camus Av 48 D5
Camus Park 48 D5
Camus Pl East 48 D5
Camus Rd East 48 D4
Camus Rd West 48 D5
Canaan La 39 E4
Candlemakers Park 51 H5
Candlemakers Row 4 D4
Canning St 25 E5
Cannon Wynd 15 H3
Canon La 25 F1
Canon St 25 F1
Canongate 5 F3
Canonmills 25 F1
Capelaw Ct 48 B3
Capelaw Rd 46 D5
Captains Dri 50 C5
Captains Loan 50 C5
Captains Rd 50 C6
Captains Row 50 D5
Carberry Pl 24 B6
Carfrae Gdns 22 D1
Carfrae Gro 23 E2
Carfrae Park 22 D1
Carfrae Rd 23 E1
Cargil Ct 14 D3
Cargil Ter 14 D3
Carlton St 24 D2
Carlton Ter 5 H1
Carlton Ter Brae 5 H1
Carlton Ter La 5 H1
Carlton Ter Mews 5 H1
Carlyle Pl 26 C2
Carmel Av 8 D3
Carmel Rd 8 D3
Carnegie Ct 5 F6
Carnethy Av 47 E5
Caroline Gdns 22 B5
Caroline Park Av 13 H2
Caroline Park Gro 13 H2
Caroline Pl 22 B5
Caroline Ter 22 A4
Carpet La 16 C3
Carrick Knowe Av 36 C1
Carrick Knowe Dri 36 C2
Carrick Knowe Gdns 36 C2
Carrick Knowe Gro 36 C2
Carrick Knowe Hill 36 C2
Carrick Knowe Loan 36 C2
Carrick Knowe Parkway 36 C2
Carrick Knowe Pl 36 C2
Carrick Knowe Rd 36 C3
Carrick Knowe Ter 36 C2
Carrington Ho 24 B1
Carrington Rd 24 B1
Carron Pl 16 D4
Carrubers Clo 5 E3
Casselbank St 16 B5
Cassells La 16 B5
Castle Av 36 B2
Castle Barnes Steps 4 A4
Castle Esplanade 4 C4
Castle Hill 4 C4
Castle St 4 A2
Castle Ter 4 A4
Castle Wynd Nth 4 C4
Castle Wynd Sth 4 C4
Castlelaw Rd 47 E5
Castleview Ho 51 G1
Cathcart Pl 24 B6
Cathedral La 5 E1
Catherine Pl 15 F6
Cattle Rd 37 F5
Cauldcoats Cotts 42 C5
Causewayside 40 A2
Cavalry Park Dri 41 F1
Chalmers Clo 5 E3
Chalmers Cres 39 G2
Chalmers St 4 C6
Chamberlain Rd 39 E3
Chambers St 4 D4
Chancelot Cres 15 F4
Chancelot Gro 15 F4
Chancelot Ter 15 G4
Chapel Ct 41 H4
Chapel La 16 C3
Chapel St 5 E6
Chapel Wynd 4 B5
Charles St 5 E6
Charles St La 4 D6
Charlesfield 5 E5
Charlotte La 25 E4
Charlotte Sq 4 A2
Charterhall Gro 39 G5
Charterhall Rd 39 G5
Cherry Tree Av 54 D2
Cherry Tree Cres 54 D2
Cherry Tree Gdns 54 D3
Cherry Tree Gro 54 D3
Cherry Tree Loan 54 D2
Cherry Tree Park 54 C3
Chessels Ct 5 F3
Chesser Av 37 F4
Chesser Cotts 37 F3
Chesser Cres 37 F4
Chesser Gdns 37 F4
Chesser Gro 37 F4
Chesser Loan 37 F4
Chester St 24 C4
Chestnut St 14 B1
Cheyne St 24 D2
Christian Cres 28 D5
Christian Gro 28 C6
Christian Path 28 C4
Christiemiller Av 27 G2
Christiemiller Gro 27 H2
Christiemiller Pl 27 H2
Church Hill 39 E3
Church Hill Dri 39 E3
Church Hill Pl 38 D3
Circus Gdns 25 E2
Circus La 25 E2
Circus Pl 25 E2
Citadel St 16 B3
City of Edinburgh
By-Pass 45 F1
Clackmae Gro 50 A2
Clackmae Rd 50 B2
Clarebank Cres 16 D5
Claremont Bank 25 G1
Claremont Ct 15 G6
Claremont Cres 15 G6
Claremont Gdns 17 E5
Claremont Gro 25 G1
Claremont Park 16 D5
Claremont Rd 16 D5
Clarence St 25 E2
Clarendon Cres 24 D3
Clarinda Ter 50 C1
Clark Av 15 F4
Clark Clo 15 E4
Clark Rd 15 E3
Claverhouse Dri 50 C2
Clayhills Gro 54 B5
Clearburn Cres 40 D3
Clearburn Gdns 40 D3
Clearburn Rd 40 D3
Cleekim Dri 42 C3
Cleekim Rd 42 C2
Cleikiminfield 42 C3
Cleikiminrig 42 C3
Clerics Hill 8 D3
Clerk St 5 F6
Clermiston Av 22 A1
Clermiston Cres 22 A2
Clermiston Dri 22 A2
Clermiston Gdns 22 A2
Clermiston Grn 22 A1
Clermiston Gro 22 B2
Clermiston Hill 22 B1
Clermiston Loan 22 A1
Clermiston Medway 22 B2
Clermiston Park 22 B1
Clermiston Pl 22 B2
Clermiston Rd 22 B6
Clermiston Rd Nth 22 B1
Clermiston Ter 22 B6
Clermiston View 22 B2
Clerwood Bank 22 A4
Clerwood Gdns 22 A4
Clerwood Gro 22 B4
Clerwood Loan 22 A4
Clerwood Park 22 A4
Clerwood Pl 22 B4
Clerwood Row 22 A4
Clerwood Ter 22 B4
Clerwood View 22 B4
Clerwood Way 22 A4
Cliftonhall Rd 9 C7
Clinton Rd 39 E3
Clockmill La 26 D3
Clovenstone Dri 46 B3
Clovenstone Gdns 46 C2
Clovenstone Park 46 C3
Clovenstone Rd 46 B1
Cloverfoot Cotts 42 C5
Cluny Av 39 E5
Cluny Dri 39 E6
Cluny Gdns 39 E5
Cluny Pl 39 F5
Cluny Ter 39 E5
Clyde St 4 D1
Clyde St Lane Nth 4 D1
Coal Hill 16 B3
Coates Cres 24 D5
Coates Gdns 24 C5
Coatfield La 16 B4
Cobbinshaw Ho 35 G6
Cobden Cres 40 B3
Cobden Rd 40 B3
Coburg St 16 A3
Cochran Pl 16 C5
Cochran Ter 25 G2
Cockburn Cres 54 A5
Cockburn Rd 54 A6
Cockburn St 4 D3
Cockmylane 48 C4
Coffin La 38 B1
Coillesdene Av 29 E5
Coillesdene Cres 29 E5
Coillesdene Dri 29 E5
Coillesdene Gdns 29 F6
Coillesdene Gro 29 E5
Coillesdene Loan 29 F5
Coillesdene Ter 29 F5
Coinyie Ho Clo 5 E4
Colinton Gro 37 H5
Colinton Gro West 38 A5
Colinton Mains Cres 48 A4
Colinton Mains Dri 48 A3
Colinton Mains Gdns 47 H2
Colinton Mains Grn 48 A3
Colinton Mains Loan 48 A3
Colinton Mains Pl 48 A3
Colinton Mains Rd 48 A3
Colinton Mains Ter 48 A3
Colinton Rd, Colinton 47 F4
Colinton Rd, Myreside 38 A5
College Wynd 5 E4
Collins Pl 25 E1
Coltbridge Av 24 A5
Coltbridge Gdns 24 A5
Coltbridge Ter 24 A5
Coltbridge Vale 24 A5
Columba Av 23 F2
Columba Rd 23 E1
Colville Pl 25 E1
Comely Bank 24 B2
Comely Bank Av 24 C2
Comely Bank Gro 24 C2
Comely Bank Pl 24 D2
Comely Bank Pl Mews 24 D2
Comely Bank Rd 24 C2
Comely Bank Row 24 D2
Comely Bank St 24 C2
Comely Bank Ter 24 C2
Comely Grn 26 C3

Street	Ref	Street	Ref	Street	Ref	Street	Ref	Street	Ref
Comely Grn Cres	26 C3	Craigleith Hill	23 H2	Crawford Rd	40 B4	Doune Ter	25 E3	Duncan Pl	
Comiston Dri	38 C6	Craigleith Hill Av	23 G1	Crewe Bank	14 A3	Dovecot Gro	47 E1	Duncan St	
Comiston Gdns	38 D6	Craigleith Hill Cres	24 A1	Crewe Cres	14 A3	Dovecot Loan	47 E1	Duncans Gait	
Comiston Gate	48 D4	Craigleith Hill Gdns	24 A2	Crewe Gro	14 A4	Dovecot Park	47 E2	Dundas Pl	
Comiston Gro	48 D3	Craigleith Hill Grn	23 H1	Crewe Loan	13 H4	Dovecot Rd	36 A1	Dundas St	36 A1
Comiston Pl	38 D6	Craigleith Hill Gro	23 H2	Crewe Pl	14 A3	Dowies Mill La	11 E5	Dundee Pl	
Comiston Rise	48 D3	Craigleith Hill Loan	24 A2	Crewe Rd Gdns	13 H4	Downfield Pl	24 B6	Dundee St	24 B6
Comiston Road	48 D2	Craigleith Hill Park	23 H1	Crewe Rd Nth	13 H3	Downie Gro	22 D6	Dundee Ter	24 B6
Comiston Spring Av	48 D3	Craigleith Hill Row	23 H2	Crewe Rd Sth	14 A5	Downie Ter	22 D6	Dundonald St	
Comiston Ter	38 D6	Craigleith Road	24 A2	Crewe Rd West	13 H3	Dreghorn Av	48 B5	Dundrennan Cotts	
Comiston View	48 C3	Craigleith View	23 G4	Crewe Ter	14 A4	Dreghorn Dri	48 A5	Dunedin St	
Commercial St	16 A3	Craiglockhart Av	37 G5	Crichton Pl	26 A1	Dreghorn Gdns	48 A5	Dunrobin Pl	
Connaught Pl	15 G4	Craiglockhart Bank	37 G6	Crichton St	5 E6	Dreghorn Gro	48 B5	Dunsmuir Ct	
Considine Gdns	27 E3	Craiglockhart Cres	47 G1	Croall Pl	26 A1	Dreghorn La	48 A5	Dunvegan Ct	
Considine Ter	27 E3	Craiglockhart Dell Rd	37 G6	Croft-an-Righ	5 H1	Dreghorn Loan	47 F4	Durar La	
Constitution Pl	16 C3	Craiglockhart Dri Nth	37 G6	Crosswood Av	54 B6	Dreghorn Park	47 H5	Durham Av	51 H4
Constitution St	16 B4	Craiglockhart Dri Sth	47 F2	Crosswood Cres	54 B5	Dreghorn Pl	48 A5	Durham Dri	
Corbiehill Av	12 D6	Craiglockhart Gdns	37 G6	Crown Pl	16 B5	Drum Av	51 H4	Durham Gdns Nth	
Corbiehill Cres	12 C6	Craiglockhart Gro	47 G1	Crown St	16 B5	Drum Brae Av	21 H4	Durham Gdns Sth	
Corbiehill Gdns	13 E6	Craiglockhart Loan	37 G6	Cuddy La	38 D4	Drum Brae Ct	21 H3	Durham Gro	
Corbiehill Gro	12 D6	Craiglockhart Park	47 G1	Cultins Rd	35 F4	Drum Brae Cres	21 H2	Durham Pl East	
Corbiehill Park	12 D6	Craiglockhart Pl	37 H5	Cumberland St	25 F2	Drum Brae Dri	21 H3	Durham Pl Lane	
Corbiehill Pl	12 C6	Craiglockhart Quadrant	47 G1	Cumin Pl	39 H2	Drum Brae Gdns	21 H4	Durham Pl West	
Corbiehill Rd	12 D6	Craiglockhart Rd	47 G2	Cumlodden Av	23 G4	Drum Brae Gro	21 H2	Durham Rd Sth	
Corbiehill Ter	12 C6	Craiglockhart Rd Nth	47 G1	Cumnor Cres	50 C1	Drum Brae Neuk	21 H3	Durham Sq	
Corbieshot	42 D2	Craiglockhart Ter	38 B5	Cunningham Pl	16 B5	Drum Brae North	21 G1	Durham Ter	
Corden Ter	24 D6	Craiglockhart Vw	37 H5	Curriehill Castle Dri	54 C2	Drum Brae Park	21 H4	Durward Gro	
Cornhill Ter	16 D5	Craigmillar Castle Av	41 F4	Curriehill Rd	55 E1	Drum Brae Park App	21 H4		
Cornwall St	4 A4	Craigmillar Castle Gdns	41 F4	Currievale Dri	54 D2	Drum Brae Pl	21 H4	Earl Grey St	
Cornwallis Pl	25 G1	Craigmillar Castle Gro	41 F4	Currievale Park	54 D2	Drum Brae South	21 H4	Earl Haig Gdns	
Coronation Walk	25 F6	Craigmillar Castle Loan	41 G3	Currievale Park Gro	54 D2	Drum Brae Ter	21 H3	Earlston Pl	
Correnie Dri	39 E6	Craigmillar Castle Rd	41 F3	Daiches Brae	43 E1	Drum Brae Walk	21 G3	East Adam St	
Correnie Gdns	39 E6	Craigmillar Castle Ter	41 F4	Daisy Ter	38 B3	Drum Cotts	51 H5	East Barnton Av	
Corslet Cres	45 F6	Craigmillar Ct	41 F4	Dalgety Av	26 D2	Drum Cres	51 H4	East Barnton Gdns	
Corslet Pl	45 F6	Craigmillar Park	40 B4	Dalgety Rd	26 D2	Drum Pl	51 H4	East Brighton Cres	
Corslet Rd	45 F6	Craigmount Av	21 H5	Dalgety St	26 D2	Drum St	51 G5	East Caystane Pl	
Corstorbank Cotts	21 H5	Craigmount Av Nth	21 G2	Dalhousie Ter	38 D6	Drum Ter	26 B1	East Caystane Rd	
Corstorphine Bank Av	21 H5	Craigmount Bank	21 G2	Dalkeith Rd	40 B1	Drum View Av	52 C3	East Castle Rd	
Corstorphine Bank Dri	22 A6	Craigmount Bank Walk	21 G3	Dalkeith St	28 D5	Drumdryan St	4 B6	East Champanyie	
Corstorphine Bank Ter	21 H6	Craigmount Bank West	21 G3	Dalmahoy Cres	54 B3	Drummond Pl	25 G2	East Clapperfield	
Corstorphine High St	36 A1	Craigmount Brae	21 G3	Dalmahoy Rd, Balerno	54 A1	Drummond St	5 E4	East Claremont St	
Corstorphine Hill Av	22 B5	Craigmount Ct	21 G2	Dalmahoy Rd, Ratho	32 B6	Drumsheugh Gdns	24 D4	East Comiston	
Corstorphine Hill Cres	22 B5	Craigmount Cres	21 G4	Dalmeny Rd	15 G4	Dryden Gdns	16 A6	East Croft	
Corstorphine Hill Gdns	22 B5	Craigmount Dri	21 G4	Dalmeny St	16 B6	Dryden Pl	40 B2	East Cromwell St	
Corstorphine Hill Rd	22 B5	Craigmount Gdns	21 G5	Dalry Pl	24 D6	Dryden St	16 A6	East Crosscauseway	
Corstorphine House Av	22 B6	Craigmount Gro	21 G5	Dalry Rd	24 C6	Dryden Ter	25 H1	East Ct, Craigmillar	
Corstorphine Park Gdns	36 B1	Craigmount Gro Nth	21 G4	Dalrymple Cres	39 H3	Drylaw Av	23 G1	East Ct, Ravelston	
Corstorphine Rd	22 C6	Craigmount Hill	21 G3	Dalziel Pl	26 D3	Drylaw Cres	23 F1	East Farm of Gilmerton	
Corunna Pl	16 B4	Craigmount Loan	21 G4	Damside	24 C4	Drylaw Gdns	23 F1	East Fettes Av	
Cotlaws	8 C3	Craigmount Park	21 G5	Danderhall Cres	52 C3	Drylaw Grn	23 F1	East Fountainbridge	
Cottage Grn	11 F4	Craigmount Pl	21 G4	Danube St	24 D2	Drylaw Gro	23 F1	East Hermitage Pl	
Cottage Homes	47 F4	Craigmount Ter	21 G5	Darnaway St	4 A1	Drylaw House Gdn	13 F6	East London St	
Cottage Park	23 E3	Craigmount View	21 G4	Darnell Rd	14 D4	Drylaw House Paddock	13 F6	East Market St	
Couper St	16 A3	Craigmount Way	21 G3	Davidson Park	14 A6	Duart Cres	21 H3	East Mayfield	
Covenant Clo	5 E3	Craigour Av	51 G1	Davidson Rd	14 A6	Dublin Meuse	25 G2	East Montgomery Pl	
Cowan Rd	38 A4	Craigour Cotts	51 H2	Davie St	5 F5	Dublin St	4 D1	East Newington Pl	
Cowanhill Rd	54 B1	Craigour Cres	51 G2	Dean Bank La	25 E2	Dublin St Lane Nth	25 G2	East Parkside	
Cowans Clo	5 F6	Craigour Dri	51 G1	Dean Bri	24 D3	Dublin St Lane Sth	4 D1	East Preston St	
Cowgate	4 D4	Craigour Gdns	51 H2	Dean Park Brae	54 B4	Duddingston Av	27 H6	*East Preston St La, East Preston St	
Cowgate Head	4 C4	Craigour Grn	51 G2	Dean Park Cres	24 D3	Duddingston Cres	28 B6	East Restalrig Ter	
Coxfield	37 G2	Craigour Gro	51 G2	Dean Park Mews	24 D2	Duddingston Gdns Nth	27 H5	East Silvermills La	
Craigcrook Av	22 D2	Craigour Loan	51 G2	Dean Park St	24 D2	Duddingston Gdns Sth	28 A6	East Suffolk Rd	
*Craigcrook Gdns, Craigcrook Rd	23 E2	Craigour Pl	51 G1	Dean Path	24 C3	Duddingston Gro East	27 H6	East Telferton	
Craigcrook Gro	23 E2	Craigour Ter	51 G2	Dean St	24 D2	Duddingston Gro West	27 H6	East Trinity Rd	
Craigcrook Park	23 E2	Craigpark Av	32 A6	Dean Ter	24 D2	Duddingston Loan	27 H6	Easter Belmont Rd	
Craigcrook Pl	23 F2	Craigpark Cres	32 A6	Deanery Clo	27 E2	Duddingston Mains Cotts	28 D6	Easter Currie Ct	
Craigcrook Rd	22 C1	Craigs Av	21 G6	Deanhaugh St	25 E2	Duddingston Mills Cotts	27 G5	Easter Currie Cres	
Craigcrook Sq	23 E2	Craigs Bank	21 G6	Deanpark Av	54 B5	Duddingston Park	28 B5	Easter Currie Pl	
Craigcrook Ter	23 F2	Craigs Cres	21 G6	Deanpark Ct	54 B5	Duddingston Park Sth	42 B1	Easter Currie Ter	
Craigend Park	51 E1	Craigs Dri	21 G5	Deanpark Cres	54 B5	Duddingston Rise	42 A1	Easter Drylaw Av	
Craigentinny Av	27 G1	Craigs Gdns	21 G6	Deanpark Gdns	54 B5	Duddingston Road	27 G6	Easter Drylaw Bank	
Craigentinny Av Nth	17 F5	Craigs Gro	21 H6	Deanpark Pl	54 B5	Duddingston Road West	41 F1	Easter Drylaw Dri	
Craigentinny Cres	27 G2	Craigs Loan	21 G5	Delhaig	37 F3	Duddingston Row	42 A1	Easter Drylaw Gdns	
Craigentinny Gro	27 G2	Craigs Park	21 G5	Dell Rd	47 E3	Duddingston Sq East	28 A6	Easter Drylaw Gro	
Craigentinny Pl	27 G2	Craigs Rd	20 B4	Denham Green Pl	15 E4	Duddingston Sq West	27 H6	Easter Drylaw Loan	
Craigentinny Rd	27 F1	Cramond Av	11 G3	Denham Green Av	15 E4	Duddingston View	42 A1	Easter Drylaw Pl	
Craighall Av	15 G3	Cramond Bank	11 G4	Derby St	15 G2	Duddingston Yd	42 B1	Easter Drylaw View	
Craighall Bank	15 G3	Cramond Cres	11 G4	Detchmont Rd	21 F6	Dudgeon Pl	8 E2	Easter Drylaw Way	
Craighall Cres	15 F3	Cramond Gdns	11 G4	Devon Pl	24 B6	Dudley Av	15 H3	Easter Haugh	
Craighall Gdns	15 F3	Cramond Glebe Gdns	11 G3	Dewar Pl	24 D5	Dudley Av Sth	15 H3	Easter Park Dri	
Craighall Rd	15 F2	Cramond Glebe Rd	11 G2	Dewar Pl La	24 D5	Dudley Bank	15 H3	Easter Park Ho	
Craighall Ter	15 F4	Cramond Glebe Ter	11 G3	Dick Pl	39 G3	Dudley Cres	15 G3	Easter Rd	
Craighill Gdns	38 C6	Cramond Grn	11 G3	Dickson St	16 B6	Dudley Gdns	15 G3	Easter Warriston	
Craighouse Av	38 B5	Cramond Gro	11 G4	Dicksons Ct	5 E4	Dudley Gro	15 G3	Eastfield Gdns	
Craighouse Gdns	38 B5	Cramond Park	11 G4	Dinmont Dri	40 D6	Duff St	24 B6	Eastfield Pl	
Craighouse Park	38 C6	Cramond Pl East	11 G3	Distillery La	24 C6	Duff Street La	24 B6	Eastfield Rd	
Craighouse Rd	38 B5	Cramond Rd Nth	11 G3	Dochart Dri	21 H3	Duke Pl	16 C5	Eastfield Ter	
Craighouse Ter	38 B6	Cramond Rd Sth	12 A3	Dock Pl	16 B3	Duke St	16 B5	Eden La	
Craigievar Sq	21 F5	Cramond Regis	11 F5	Dock St	16 B3	Dukes Walk	26 D3	Edina Pl	
Craigievar Wynd	21 F5	Cramond Ter	11 G4	Dolphin Av	55 E2	Dumbiedykes Rd	5 G4	Edina St	
Craiglea Dri	38 C6	Cramond Vale	11 F4	Dolphin Gdns East	55 E2	Dumbryden Dri	36 C6	Edinburgh Rd, Cramond Bridge	
Craiglea Pl	38 B6	Cramond Village	11 G2	Dolphin Gdns West	55 E2	Dumbryden Gdns	36 C6	Edinburgh Rd, Newbridge	
Craigleith Av Nth	23 G3	Cranston St	5 F3	Dolphin Rd	55 E2	Dumbryden Gro	46 C1	Edmonstone Av	
Craigleith Av Sth	23 G4	Crarae Av	24 A4	Dorset Pl	38 C1	Dumbryden Rd	46 C1	Edmonstone Rd	
Craigleith Bank	23 G3	Craufordland	11 F6	Double Hedges Park	50 C1	Dunard Gdns	39 G4	Edmonstone Ter	
Craigleith Cres	23 G2			Double Hedges Rd	50 C1	Dunbar St	4 A6	Eglinton Cres	
Craigleith Dri	23 G3			Douglas Cres	24 C5	Dunbars Clo	5 G3		
Craigleith Gdns	23 G3			Douglas Gdns	24 C4				
Craigleith Gro	23 G3			Douglas Ter	24 C6				

‖ St	24 B6
ews	39 F5
t	15 E6
er	15 E6
	16 C4
er	28 D4
	4 D1
East	4 D1
Pl	28 B2
	24 B6
Nth	26 B1
Sth	26 B2
r	26 B2
d	15 H5
wan Ter	41 E6
len Loan	51 E3
len Rd	51 E3
d	51 E4
y Rd	23 F5
ns	47 G2
rk	47 G2
	47 G2
	47 G2
	26 B1
	16 C5
	25 H2
d Ter	16 D6
am Gdns	37 G3
am Gro	37 G3
am Ter	37 G3
	39 G3
de	11 H2
de Ter	29 E5
an Pl	22 A3
an Ter	22 A3
ae	11 E5
ark	11 E5
	11 E5
nt Rd	40 B5
r	38 D6
	24 D3
le Pl	25 E1
ro	38 D2
d	38 C3
	39 H5
s	25 F1
	25 F1
	25 F1
ar	11 F4
ar Cotts	11 G3
Gdns	40 D6
Av	49 E5
Rd	18 D6
	50 D5
v	39 E4
t	39 E4
dns	39 E4
d	39 E4
d West	39 E4
Gdns	22 B3
ro	27 H3
er	27 H3
rn	21 F2
all Av	22 A6
all Cres North	22 A6
all Cres South	22 A6
all Gro	22 A6
all Pl	22 A6
all Rd	22 A6
all Ter	22 A6
ll Av	51 G4
ll Dri	51 H4
ll Gdns	51 H4
ll Gro	51 H3
ll Pl	51 H4
ll Rd	51 G4
ll Sq	51 H4
ll St	51 H4
ll Ter	51 H4
ll Way	51 H3
v Av	46 D5
v Gdns	46 D6
de Av	51 H3
de Cres	51 G3
de Dri	51 H3
de Gro	51 G3
de Gro	51 H3
Av	13 G5
Dri	13 H3
Gdns	13 G5
Gro	13 G5
Pl	13 G5
Bangholm	15 E4
Drylaw	13 E6
d	14 C4
Sq	4 A4
y	24 B1
se	14 C5
ow	25 F2

Fidra Ct	13 E4
Figgate Bank	28 C3
Figgate La	28 C3
Figgate St	28 B3
Fillyside Av	27 G1
Fillyside Rd	17 G6
Fillyside Ter	27 G1
Findhorn Pl	40 A2
Findlay Av	27 E1
Findlay Cotts	17 E6
Findlay Gdns	17 E6
Findlay Gro	27 F1
Findlay Medway	17 E6
Fingal Pl	39 G1
Fingzies Pl	16 D5
Firrhill Cres	48 A2
Firrhill Dri	48 B3
Firrhill Loan	48 A3
First Gait	44 D2
Fish Market Sq	15 G2
Fishers Ct	4 D4
Fishwives Causeway	27 G3
Fleshmarket Ct	5 E3
Forbes Rd	39 E2
Forbes St	5 G6
Fords Rd	37 F3
Forres St	4 A1
Forrest Hill	4 D5
Forrest Rd	4 D5
Forrester Park Av	36 A3
Forrester Park Dri	36 A3
Forrester Park Gdns	36 A3
Forrester Park Grn	36 B3
Forrester Park Gro	36 B3
Forrester Park Loan	36 B3
Forsyths Clo	5 G2
Fort Ho	15 H3
Forteviot Ho	51 F2
Forth Av	55 E2
Forth Gait	44 C3
Forth St	25 H2
Forth View Cres, Currie	55 E1
Forth View Cres, Danderhall	52 C2
Forth View Rd	55 E2
Forthview Rd	23 F1
Forthview Ter	23 F2
Foulis Cres	46 B4
Fountain Clo	5 E3
Fountainbridge	4 A6
Fountainhall Rd	39 H4
Fowler Ter	38 C1
Fox Covert Av	22 B3
Fox Covert Gro	22 B3
Fox Spring Cres	48 C4
Fox Spring Rise	48 C4
Fraser Av	14 C4
Fraser Cres	14 C4
Fraser Gdns	14 D4
Fraser Gro	14 C4
Frederick St	4 B2
Freelands Rd	32 C5
Freer St	25 E5
Frogston Av	49 E6
Frogston Gdns	49 E6
Frogston Rd East	50 A6
Frogston Rd West	49 E6
Frogston Ter	49 F5
Gabriels Rd, Edinburgh	4 D2
Gabriels Rd, Stockbridge	25 E1
Galachlawshot	49 G5
Galachlawside	49 G5
Galloways Entry	5 G2
Gamekeepers Loan	11 G4
Gamekeepers Park	11 F4
Gamekeepers Rd	11 F4
Gamekeepers Way	11 H3
Garden Ter	12 B5
Gardiner Gro	23 F2
Gardiner Rd	23 E2
Gardiner Ter	23 E2
Gardners Cres	24 D5
Garscube Ter	23 H4
Garvald Ct	50 D5
Gateside Rd	8 C3
Gayfield Pl La	25 H2
Gayfield Sq	25 H2
Gayfield St	25 H2
Gayfield St La	25 H2
Geddes Entry	5 E3
George IV Bri	4 D4
George Sq	4 D6
George Sq La	4 D6
George St	4 A2
Gibson St	15 H5
Gibson Ter	38 C1

Gifford Pl	25 H6
Gilberstoun	43 E1
Gilberstoun Pl	43 E1
Giles St, Edinburgh	4 D3
Giles St, Leith	16 B4
Gillespie Cres	39 E1
Gillespie Pl	39 E1
Gillespie Rd	46 C4
Gillespie St	39 E1
Gillsland Park	38 C3
Gillsland Rd	38 B3
Gilmerton Dykes Av	51 F5
Gilmerton Dykes Cres	51 E5
Gilmerton Dykes Dri	51 F4
Gilmerton Dykes Gdns	51 E5
Gilmerton Dykes Gro	51 E5
Gilmerton Dykes Loan	51 F6
Gilmerton Dykes Pl	51 E5
Gilmerton Dykes Rd	51 F6
Gilmerton Dykes St	51 E5
Gilmerton Dykes Ter	51 F6
Gilmerton Dykes View	51 F5
Gilmerton Rd	50 D1
Gilmerton Station Rd	52 A6
Gilmore Park	38 D1
Gilmore Pl	38 D1
Gilmour Rd	40 B4
Gilmours Entry	5 F6
Gilmours St	5 F6
*Gladstone Ct, Bowling Green Clo	5 F3
Gladstone Pl	16 D5
Gladstone Ter	39 H1
Glasgow Rd, Gogar	34 A2
Glasgow Rd, Newbridge	9 E6
Glasgow Rd, Ratho	32 A1
Glasgow Rd, West Craigs	21 E6
Glebe Gdns	22 B6
Glebe Gro	11 B6
Glebe Rd	22 B6
Glebe Ter	22 B6
Glen St	4 B6
Glenallan Dri	40 D6
Glenallen Loan	41 E6
Glenalmond Ct	36 A5
Glenbrook Rd	54 A5
Glencairn Cres	24 C5
Glendevon Av	37 E1
Glendevon Gdns	37 E1
Glendevon Gro	37 E1
Glendevon Park	37 F1
Glendevon Pl	37 F1
Glendevon Rd	37 E1
Glendevon Ter	37 E1
Glendinning Cres	50 C2
Glenfinlas St	25 E3
Glengyle Ter	39 E1
Glenisla Gdns	39 G5
Glenisla Gdns La	39 G5
Glenlea Cotts	37 G3
Glenlee Av	27 E3
Glenlee Gdns	27 E4
Glenlockhart Bank	37 H6
Glenlockhart Rd	48 A1
Glenlockhart Valley	37 H6
Glenogle Ho	25 E1
Glenogle Pl	25 E1
Glenogle Rd	25 E1
Glenogle Ter	25 E1
Glenorchy Ter	40 B3
Glenure Loan	22 A3
Glenvarloch Cres	50 C1
Gloucester La	4 A1
Gloucester Pl	25 E2
Gloucester Sq	4 A1
Gloucester St	25 E2
Goff Av	28 A2
Gogar Station Rd	34 B1
Gogarbank	34 C5
Gogarloch Haugh	35 F2
Gogarloch Muir	35 F2
Gogarloch Rd	35 F2
Gogarloch Syke	35 F2
Gogarside Roundabout	34 D1
Goggar Mains Farm Rd	34 A1
Goldenacre Ter	15 E5
Gordon Ct	16 C5
Gordon Loan	22 C6
Gordon St	16 B5
Gordon Ter	40 C6
Gorgie Cotts	37 G2
Gorgie Rd	37 F4
Gosford Pl	15 G4
Gracemount Av	50 C4
Gracemount Dri	50 C4
Gracemount Pl	50 D4
Gracemount Rd	50 C6
Gracemount Sq	50 C4

Graham St	15 H4
Granby Rd	40 B4
Grandville	15 F3
Grange Cres	39 H3
Grange Loan	39 F3
Grange Loan Gdns	39 G3
Grange Rd	39 G2
Grange Ter	39 G4
Grant Av	47 E5
Granton Av	14 B2
Granton Cres	14 B2
Granton Gdns	14 C3
Granton Gro	14 C3
Granton Mains Av	13 G3
Granton Mains Vale	13 G3
Granton Mains Wynd	13 G3
Granton Medway	14 B2
Granton Park	14 A2
Granton Pl	14 C3
Granton Rd	14 C2
Granton Neuk	14 C2
Granton Sq	14 B2
Granton Ter	14 C2
Granton View	14 B2
Grantully Pl	40 B2
Granville Ter	38 D2
Grassmarket	4 C4
Grays Loan	38 B4
Great Cannon Bank	28 B2
Great Carleton Sq	42 B4
Great Junction St	16 A3
Great King St	25 F2
Great Michael Rise	15 G2
Great Stuart Pl	25 E3
Green Loan	50 D1
Green St	25 H1
Greenbank Av	48 D1
Greenbank Cres	48 C3
Greenbank Dri	48 C1
Greenbank Gdns	48 C2
Greenbank Gro	48 C2
Greenbank La	48 C1
Greenbank Loan	48 C1
Greenbank Park	48 C2
Greenbank Pl	48 D1
Greenbank Rise	48 C3
Greenbank Road	48 C2
Greenbank Row	48 C2
Greendykes Av	41 H4
Greendykes Dri	41 H5
Greendykes Gdns	42 A5
Greendykes Ho	42 A5
Greendykes Loan	41 H4
Greendykes Rd	41 H4
Greendykes Ter	41 H4
Greenend Dri	51 E3
Greenend Gdns	51 E3
Greenend Gro	51 E2
Greenfield Cres	54 B6
Greenfield Rd	54 B6
Greenhill Gdns	39 E2
Greenhill Park	39 E3
Greenhill Pl	39 E2
Greenhill Ter	39 E2
Greenlaw Hedge	48 B3
Greenlaw Rig	48 B3
Greenside La	25 H2
Greenside Row	5 F1
Greigs Hill	8 D3
Greyfriars Pl	4 D5
Grierson Av	14 C3
Grierson Cres	14 C3
Grierson Gdns	14 C3
Grierson Rd	14 C3
Grierson Sq	14 C3
Grierson Villas	14 C3
Grigor Av	14 A6
Grigor Dri	14 A6
Grigor Gdns	14 A6
Grigor Ter	14 A6
Grindlay St	4 A5
Grindlay St Ct	4 A5
Groathill Av	23 G1
Groathill Gdns East	23 G1
Groathill Gdns West	23 G1
Groathill Rd Nth	13 F5
Groathill Rd Sth	23 G1
Grosvenor Cres	24 C5
Grosvenor Gdns	24 C5
Grosvenor St	24 C5
Grove St	24 D5
Grove Ter	24 D5
Guardians Wood	23 G5
Gullans Clo	5 F3
Gunnet Ct	13 E4
Guthrie St	5 E4
Gyle Park Gdns	35 F1
Gylemuir Rd	21 H6
Haddington Pl	26 A2
Haddon Ct	5 F6

Hailes App	47 E3
Hailes Av	47 E2
Hailes Bank	46 D3
Hailes Cres	47 E3
Hailes Gdns	46 D3
Hailes Gro	46 D3
Hailes Park	46 D3
Hailes St	39 E1
Hailes Ter	46 D3
Hailesland Gdns	46 B1
Hailesland Gro	46 B1
Hailesland Park	46 C1
Hailesland Pl	46 C1
Hailesland Rd	46 B1
Hainburn Park	48 B6
Hallcroft Clo	32 A5
Hallcroft Cres	32 A5
Hallcroft Gdns	32 B4
Hallcroft Grn	32 A5
Hallcroft Neuk	32 A5
Hallcroft Park	32 A6
Hallcroft Rise	32 A6
Hallhead Rd	40 B6
Hallyard Rd	32 D1
Hallyards Rd	8 D4
Halmyre St	16 B6
Hamilton Dri	28 A5
Hamilton Dri West	27 H5
Hamilton Gdns	27 H5
Hamilton Gro	27 H5
Hamilton Park	28 A5
Hamilton Pl	25 E2
Hamilton Ter	28 B5
Hamilton Wynd	15 H3
Hampton Pl	24 B5
Hampton Ter	24 B5
Hanmuir Side	37 E6
Hannahfield	54 A4
Hanover St	4 C1
Harbour Pl	28 B3
Harbour Rd, Granton	14 B1
Harbour Rd, Portobello	28 B3
Harden Pl	38 C2
Harelaw Rd	47 E5
Harewood Cres	41 G3
Harewood Dri	41 G3
Harewood Rd	41 G3
Harlaw March	54 C6
Harlaw Rd	54 C5
Harrison Gdns	38 B3
Harrison La	38 B2
Harrison Pl	38 B3
Harrison Rd	38 B2
Hart St	25 H2
Hart St La	25 H2
Hartington Gdns	38 D2
Hartington Pl	38 D2
Harvest Dri	9 E7
Harvest Rd	9 D7
Harwell Clo	5 F6
Hasties Clo	5 F6
Hatton Pl	39 G2
Haugh Park	37 E5
Haugh St	25 E2
Hawkhead Cres	50 B3
Hawkhead Gro	50 C3
Hawkhill Av	26 C1
Hawthornbank Pl	15 H3
Hawthornbank Ter	15 H3
Hawthorne Bank La	24 C4
Hawthorne Pl	51 G5
Hawthornvale	15 G2
Hay Av	42 A2
Hay Dri	42 B2
Hay Pl	42 A2
Hay Rd	42 A3
Hay Ter	42 A3
Hayfield	21 F4
Haymarket	24 C5
Haymarket Ter	24 C5
Hazelbank Ter	38 A3
Hazledean Ter	40 D6
Hazlewood Gro	41 E6
Headrigg Row	40 D6
Helen St	16 A3
Henderland Rd	23 H5
Henderson Gdns	16 B4
Henderson Pl	25 E1
Henderson Row	25 E1
Henderson St	16 B4
Henderson Ter	38 B1
Heriot Bri	4 C4
Heriot Cross	4 C6
Heriot Hill Ter	25 G1
Heriot Pl	4 C5
Heriot Row	4 A1
Herman Cres	38 A3
Hermand St	38 A3
Hermand Ter	38 A3

Name	Ref	Name	Ref	Name	Ref	Name	Ref	Name
Hermiston Ct	36 A5	Howe St	4 B1	Jeffrey St	4 E3	Lady Wynd	4 B5	Liston Pl
Hermiston Gait	35 F5	Hugh Miller Pl	24 D1	Jessfield Ter	15 G2	Ladycroft	54 C4	Liston Rd
Hermiston House Rd	34 B6	Humbie Rd	8 D2	John St	28 D4	Ladysmith Rd	39 H5	Little France Ho
Hermiston Walk	44 D2	Hunter Sq	5 E3	John St La	28 D4	Ladywell Av	36 A1	Little Rd
Hermitage Dri	39 E6	Huntley St	25 F1	Johns La	16 C4	Ladywell Gdns	36 A1	Livingstone Pl
Hermitage Gdns	39 E6	Hutchison Av	37 G4	Johns Pl	16 C4	Ladywell Rd	36 A1	Lixmount Av
Hermitage Park	16 C6	Hutchison Cotts	37 G4	Johnsburn Grn	54 B5	Laichpark Pl	37 F4	Lixmount Gdns
Hermitage Park Gro	16 D6	Hutchison Crossway	37 G3	Johnsburn Haugh	54 A5	Laichpark Rd	37 F4	Loanhead Rd
Hermitage Park Sth	16 D6	Hutchison Gdns	37 G4	Johnsburn Park	54 A5	Laing Ter	28 D4	Loaning Cres
Hermitage Pl	16 C5	Hutchison Gro	37 H3	Johnsburn Rd	54 A5	Lambs Clo	5 F6	Loaning Rd
Hermitage Ter	39 E5	Hutchison Ho	37 H3	Johnston Ter	4 B4	*Lambs Ct, Main St	15 G2	Loch Rd
High Buckstone	49 F5	Hutchison Loan	37 G4	Jollies Clo	4 C4	Lammermoor Ter	51 E1	Lochend
High Riggs	4 B6	Hutchison Medway	37 G3	Joppa Gdns	29 E5	Lampacre Rd	36 C1	Lochend Av
High School Yds	5 F4	Hutchison Park	37 G3	Joppa Gro	28 D5	Lanark Rd	46 A5	Lochend Clo
High St, Edinburgh	4 D4	Hutchison Pl	37 G4	Joppa Pans	29 F5	Lanark Rd West	54 A4	Lochend Cres
High St, Kirkliston	8 D3	Hutchison Rd	37 G4	Joppa Park	29 E5	Lane East	25 G2	Lochend Dri
Highlea Circle	54 B6	Hutchison Ter	37 G4	Joppa Rd	28 D5	Lane West	25 G2	Lochend Gdns
Highlea Gro	54 B6	Hutchison View	37 G3	Joppa Ter	28 D5	Langton Rd	40 A4	Lochend Gro
Hill Pl	5 E5	Hyndfords Clo	5 E3	Jordan La	39 E5	Lansdowne Cres	24 A5	Lochend Ho
Hill Sq	5 F5	Hyvot Av	51 F4	Jubilee Rd	19 E5	Lansdowne Ho	24 A5	Lochend Park
Hill St	4 B2	Hyvot Bank Av	51 G5	Junction Pl	16 B4	Lapicide Pl	15 H3	Lochend Quadrant
Hill St La Nth	4 B2	Hyvot Ct	51 G6	Juniper Av	46 A5	Larbour Field	46 A1	Lochend Rd
Hill St La Sth	4 B2	Hyvot Dri	51 G5	Juniper Gdns	45 H5	Larchfield	54 B4	Lochend Rd Sth
Hill View	23 F2	Hyvot Gdns	51 G5	Juniper Gro	46 A5	Larchfield Neuk	54 B4	Lochend Sq
Hillcoat Loan	28 B2	Hyvot Grn	51 G5	Juniper Park Rd	46 A4	Largo Pl	16 A3	Lochrin Pl
Hillcoat Pl	28 B2	Hyvot Gro	51 G5	Juniper Ter	46 A5	Lasswade Bank	51 E6	Lochrin Ter
Hillhouse Rd	22 C1	Hyvot Loan	51 F4			Lasswade Gro	51 E5	Lochview Ct
Hillpark Av	22 C1	Hyvot Park	51 G5	Kaimes View	52 C3	Lasswade Rd	50 D3	Lockerby Cotts
Hillpark Brae	22 D2	Hyvot Ter	51 F5	Kaims Rd	22 C5	Lauder Loan	39 H3	Lockerby Cres
Hillpark Ct	22 D1	Hyvot View	51 G6	Katesmill Rd	47 E2	Lauder Rd	39 G2	Lockerby Gro
Hillpark Cres	22 D1			Kedslie Pl	50 B3	Lauderdale St	39 F2	Lockharton Av
Hillpark Dri	22 C1	Inchgarvie Ct	13 H4	Kedslie Rd	50 B3	Laurel Ter	38 B2	Lockharton Cres
Hillpark Gdns	22 C1	Inchkeith Ct	26 A1	Keir St	4 C5	Laurie St	16 B4	Lockharton Gdns
Hillpark Grn	22 D2	Inchmickery Ct	12 D4	Keith Cres	23 F2	Lauriston Farm Rd	12 C5	Logan St
Hillpark Gro	22 C2	Inchview Ter	28 A2	Keith Row	23 F2	Lauriston Gdns	4 B6	Loganlea Av
Hillpark Loan	22 D1	India Bldgs	4 D4	Keith Ter	23 F2	Lauriston Park	4 B6	Loganlea Dri
Hillpark Rd	22 C1	India Pl	25 E2	Kekewich Av	27 H2	Lauriston Pl	4 B6	Loganlea Gdns
Hillpark Ter	22 C2	India St	25 E2	Kemp Pl	25 E1	Lauriston St	4 B5	Loganlea Loan
Hillpark View	22 C2	INDUSTRIAL ESTATES:		Kenilworth Dri	50 C2	Lauriston Ter	4 C5	Loganlea Pl
Hillpark Way	22 D1	Baileyfield Ind Est	28 B3	Kenmure Av	27 E3	Laverockbank Av	15 F2	Loganlea Rd
Hillpark Wood	23 E1	Blinkbonny Ind Est	55 G1	Kerr St	25 E2	Laverockbank Av Sth	15 F2	Loganlea Ter
Hillside Cres	26 A2	Bonnington Ind Est	15 H4	Kilgraston Rd	39 G3	Laverockbank Cres	15 F2	Logie Green Gdns
Hillside Rd	10 B4	Broadway Park	35 G3	Kilmaurs Rd	40 C2	Laverockbank Gdns	15 F2	Logie Green Loan
Hillside St	26 A2	Cameron Toll		Kilmaurs Ter	40 C3	Laverockbank Gro	15 F3	Logie Green Rd
Hilltown Ter	52 D1	· Shopping Centre	40 C5	Kimmershame Ho	24 B1	Laverockbank Rd	15 F2	Lomond Rd
Hillview Cotts	32 B6	Castlebrae		Kinellan Rd	23 F4	Laverockbank Ter	15 F2	London Rd
Hillview Cres	22 A5	Bus. Centre	41 G3	King Edwards Way	8 C3	Laverockdale	47 F5	London St
Hillview Dri	21 H5	Clifton Trading Est	9 C8	King St, Greenside	5 E1	Laverockdale Loan	47 F5	Long Dalmahoy Rd
Hillview Rd	22 A5	Craigleith Ind Est	23 H1	King St, South Leith	16 B4	Laverockdale Park	47 F6	Longformacus Rd
Hillview Ter	22 A5	Edinburgh Park Business		Kinghorn Pl	15 G4	Law Pl	28 B3	Longstone Av
Hillwood Av	32 A2	& Techology Park	34 D3	Kings Cramond	11 G4	Lawnmarket	4 D4	Longstone Cotts
Hillwood Cres	32 A1	Edinburgh West		Kings Haugh	41 E3	Leadervale Rd	50 B2	Longstone Cres
Hillwood Gdns	32 A1	Office Park	35 E2	Kings Pl	28 B2	Leadervale Ter	50 A2	Longstone Gdns
Hillwood Rise	32 A1	Jenners Depository	37 F1	Kings Rd	28 B2	Leamington Pl	39 E1	Longstone Gro
Hillwood Road	32 A1	Kings Haugh Ind Est	41 F3	Kings Stables La	4 B5	Leamington Rd	38 D1	Longstone Park
Hillwood Ter	32 A1	Kinnaird Park	42 D3	Kings Stables Rd	4 A4	Leamington Ter	38 D1	Longstone Rd
Hollybank Ter	38 A3	Lochend Ind Est	9 E7	Kings Ter	28 A2	Learmonth Av	24 C2	Longstone St
Holyrood Ct	5 G4	Newbridge Ind Est	9 B7	Kingsburgh Rd	23 G5	Learmonth Cres	24 C2	Longstone Ter
Holyrood Park Rd	40 B1	Peffermill Ind Est	41 F3	Kingsknowe Av	46 D1	Learmonth Gdns	24 C2	Longstone View
Holyrood Rd	5 F4	Roddinglaw		Kingsknowe Ct	46 D1	Learmonth Gdns La	24 C2	Lonsdale Ter
Home St	4 A6	Trading Est	33 C4	Kingsknowe Cres	46 D1	Learmonth Gdns Mews	24 D2	Lorne Pl
Hope La	28 C4	Sighthill Ind Est	35 G5	Kingsknowe Dri	46 D1	Learmonth Gro	24 C2	Lorne Sq
Hope Park Cres	39 H1	South Gyle Ind Est	35 G3	Kingsknowe Gdns	47 E2	Learmonth Park	24 C2	Lorne St
Hope Park Sq	25 H6	West One Bus. Park	35 F5	Kingsknowe Gro	47 E2	Learmonth Pl	24 C2	Lothian Rd
Hope Park Ter	39 H1	Industrial Rd	16 C5	Kingsknowe Park	47 E1	Learmonth Ter	24 C3	Lothian St
Hope St	25 E4	Industry La	15 H3	Kingsknowe Pl	36 D6	Learmonth Ter Loan	24 C3	Lovedale Av
Hope St La	4 A3	Infirmary St	5 E4	Kingsknowe Rd Nth	36 D6	Learmonth View	24 C3	Lovedale Cres
Hope Ter	39 F3	Inglewood Pl	50 D1	Kingsknowe Rd Sth	46 D1	Lee Cres	28 C4	Lovedale Gdns
Hopefield Ter	16 A3	Inglis Green Rd	37 E5	Kingsknowe Ter	47 E1	Leith St	5 E2	Lovedale Gro
Hopetoun Cres	25 H1	Inveralmond Dri	11 F4	Kingston Av	51 E1	Leith Walk	25 H2	Lovedale Rd
Hopetoun Cres La	25 H1	Inveralmond Gdns	11 F4	Kinnear Rd	14 C5	Lennox Row	14 D2	Lower Gilmore Pl
Hopetoun St	25 H1	Inveralmond Gro	11 F4	Kirk Brae	50 C1	Lennox St	24 D3	Lower Granton Rd
Horne Ter	38 D1	Inverleith Av	14 D4	Kirk Cramond	11 G2	Lennox Street La	24 D3	Lower Joppa
Horsburgh Bank	54 B3	Inverleith Av Sth	15 E5	Kirk Loan	22 B6	Lennymuir	19 G3	Lower London Rd
Horsburgh Gdns	54 B3	Inverleith Gdns	14 D4	Kirk Park	50 C2	Leslie Pl	24 D2	Lumsden Ct
Horsburgh Gro	54 B3	Inverleith Gro	14 C6	Kirk St	16 B5	Leven St	39 E1	Lussielaw Rd
Horse Wynd	5 H2	Inverleith Pl	14 C6	Kirkgate, Currie	55 F2	Leven Ter	39 F1	Lutton Pl
Hoseason Gdns	22 A3	Inverleith Pl Lane	15 E5	Kirkgate, Liberton	50 C3	Lewis Ter	24 C6	Lygon Rd
Hosie Rigg	42 C1	Inverleith Row	15 E4	Kirkhill Dri	40 C3	Liberton Brae	50 C2	Lyne St
House o'Hill Av	13 E6	Inverleith Ter	15 E6	Kirkhill Gdns	40 C2	Liberton Dri	50 A2	Lynedoch Pl La
House o'Hill Brae	13 E6	Inverleith Ter La	25 F1	Kirkhill Rd	40 C2	Liberton Gdns	50 C5	Lyons Clo
House o'Hill Cres	23 E1	Iona St	26 B1	Kirkhill Ter	40 C2	Liberton Rd	40 C6	
House o'Hill Gdns	23 E1	Ivanhoe Cres	50 D1	Kirklands	36 A2	Lidd Pl	25 F1	McDonald Pl
House o'Hill Grn	23 E1	Ivy Ter	38 A2	Kirkliston Rd	9 C5	Lidgate Shot	32 C6	McDonald Rd
House o'Hill Gro	13 E6			Kirkstyle Gdns	8 D3	Lillyhill Ter	27 E3	McDonald St
House o'Hill Pl	13 E6	Jacksons Clo	5 E3	Kirkstyle Rd	8 D3	Lily Ter	38 B3	Macdowall Rd
House o'Hill Rd	13 E6	Jamaica Mews	4 A1	Klondyke St	43 F3	Lindean Pl	16 D5	Mackenzie Pl
House o'Hill Row	23 E1	Jamaica St	4 A1	Klondyke Way	43 F3	Lindsay Pl	16 A3	McLaren Rd
House o'Hill Ter	23 F2	Jamaica St North La	4 A1	Kyle Pl	26 B3	Lindsay Rd	15 G5	McLaren Ter
Howard Pl	15 F6	Jamaica St South La	4 A1			Lindsay St	15 H3	McLeod St
Howden Hall Ct	50 A5	James Ct	4 C4	Ladehead	15 G5	Links Gdns	16 D4	McNeills Pl
Howden Hall Cres	50 B5	James Craig Walk	5 E2	Ladiemeadow	36 B2	Links Gdns La	16 D4	Madeira Pl
Howden Hall Gdns	50 C5	James St	16 A6	Lady Lawson St	4 B5	Links La	16 C4	Madeira St
Howden Hall Dri	50 B5	James St La	28 D4	Lady Menzies Pl	26 C2	Links Pl	16 C4	Magdala Cres
Howden Hall Loan	50 B5	Jameson Pl	16 B6	Lady Nairne Cres	27 F6	Links View Ho	16 B4	Magdala Mews
Howden Hall Park	50 B5	Jane St	16 B5	Lady Nairne Gro	27 F5	Lismore Av	27 E3	Magdalene Av
Howden Hall Rd	50 C5	Janefield	53 B1	Lady Nairne Loan	27 F5	Lismore Cres	27 E3	Magdalene Ct
Howden Hall Way	50 B5	Jawbone Walk	39 G1	Lady Nairne Pl	27 F5	Liston Dri	8 D2	Magdalene Dri
Howden St	5 F6	Jean Armour Av	50 C1	Lady Rd	40 C5			Magdalene Gdns
Howe Park	48 B6	Jeffrey Av	23 F2	Lady Stairs Clo	4 D3			Magdalene Loan

72

alene Medway 42 C1
alene Pl 28 C6
ncraig Ct 23 G2
ncraig Cres 23 G2
ncraig Gro 23 G2
Point 4 B5
St, Balerno 54 C4
St,
idson's Main 12 C6
St, Kirkliston 8 C2
St, Newhaven 15 G2
St, Ratho 32 B6
and Hog La 8 D4
and Rd 8 D2
ny 54 C6
ny Av 54 C5
Ter 25 E2
erston Ct 16 B5
erston St 16 B5
ering Pl 50 D2
r Pl 24 C4
e Rd, Corstorphine 22 A6
e Rd, Kirkliston 8 D3
e St 22 A6
field Pl 25 G2
field Rd 54 C5
ionhouse Rd 39 G2
n Gro 22 D1
n Pines 22 D1
n Rd 22 D1
nbank Dri 54 B6
nbank Gdns 54 B5
nbank Gro 54 B6
nbank Pl 54 B5
nbank Way 54 B5
nfield Gro 22 D1
nfield Park 22 D1
nfield Park La 12 C6
nfield Rd 22 D1
nhall Cres 40 C2
nhall Pl 40 B2
nhall Rd 40 C2
imont Cres 39 G1
imont Rd 39 F1
imont St 39 F1
nle Cres 38 C3
e Dri 12 B2
e Esplanade 17 E3
e Par 16 A2
nville Av 27 E2
nville Cres 27 E2
nville Dri 27 E2
nville Gro 27 E2
nville Park 26 D2
nville Rd 26 C2
me La 16 C3
me St 16 C4
t St 4 C3
orough St 28 C4
ion Cres 40 D6
all Rd 8 D3
all St 5 E5
alls Ct 5 F1
lo Ct 13 E4
ll Clo 5 F6
Tree Ho 51 G2
eld, Abbeyhill 26 B2
eld, Portobello 28 C3
eld Pl 26 B2
ford Av 52 C3
ce Pl 39 H5
ell St 38 D5
t 13 E4
iry Dri 21 E4
iry Rd 21 E4
eld Gdns 40 B3
eld Gdns La 40 B3
eld Pl 22 A6
eld Rd 40 A3
eld Ter 40 B3
le Gdns 15 F2
w La 25 H6
w Pl 39 G1
w Pl Rd 35 H1
w Rd 44 D3
wbank 26 D3
wbank Av 27 E3
wbank Cres 27 E3
wbank Pl 27 E3
wbank Ter 26 D3
wfield Av 27 G5
wfield Dri 27 G5
wfield Gdns 27 F6
wfield Ter 20 C5
27 F6
whouse Rd 36 B1
wspot 38 B5
side 21 F4
n Ho 35 H6

Meggetland Ter 38 A5
Melgund Ter 25 G1
Mellis Park 27 G3
Melville Cres 24 D4
Melville Dri 39 F1
Melville St 24 D4
Melville St La, Dean 24 D4
Melville St La, Portobello 28 C4
Melville Ter 39 H1
Mentone Av 28 C3
Mentone Gdns 40 B4
Mentone Ter 40 B4
Merchant St 4 D4
Merchiston Av 38 C1
Merchiston Bank Av 38 D3
Merchiston Bank Gdns 38 D3
Merchiston Cres 38 C3
Merchiston Gdns 38 B4
Merchiston Gro 38 A2
Merchiston Mews 38 C1
Merchiston Park 38 D2
Merchiston Pl 38 D2
Mertoun Pl 38 C2
Meuse La 4 D2
Mid Liberton 40 C6
Mid New Cultins 35 F5
Middle Gillsland Rd 38 C3
Middle Meadow Walk 4 D6
Middle Pier 14 C1
Middleby St 40 A3
Middlefield 26 A1
Midmar Av 39 F5
Midmar Dri 39 F6
Midmar Gdns 39 E6
Mill La 16 A3
Millar Cres 38 D5
Millar Pl 38 D5
Millar Pl La 38 D5
Miller Row 24 D3
Millerfield Pl 39 H1
Millerhill Rd 42 C5
Millgate 54 D6
Milnes Ct 4 C3
Milton Dri 29 F5
Milton Gdns Nth 28 B6
Milton Gdns Sth 42 B1
Milton Gro 29 F5
Milton Link 28 D6
Milton Rd 28 B6
Milton Rd East 29 E6
Milton Rd West 27 G6
Milton St 26 C3
Milton Ter 29 F5
Minacre 15 G4
Minto St 40 A2
Mitchell St 16 C4
Moat Dri 37 H3
Moat Pl 37 H3
Moat St 37 H3
Moat Ter 37 H3
Moira Park 27 H3
Moira Ter 27 G3
Moncreiffe Ho 51 F2
Monkwood Ct 39 G3
Monmouth Ter 15 E4
Montagu Ter 15 E4
Montague St 40 A1
Montcrieff Ter 39 H1
Montgomery St 26 A2
Montgomery St Lane 26 A2
Montpelier 38 D2
Montpelier Park 38 D2
Montpelier Ter 38 D2
Montrose Ter 26 B2
Moorfield Cotts 52 D2
Moray Pl 25 E3
Moredun Dykes Rd 51 G5
Moredun Ho 51 G2
Moredun Park Ct 51 F3
Moredun Park Dri 51 F3
Moredun Park Gdns 51 F3
Moredun Park Grn 51 G3
Moredun Park Gro 51 G4
Moredun Park Loan 51 G3
Moredun Park Rd 51 F3
Moredun Park St 51 G3
Moredun Park View 51 G4
Moredun Park Walk 51 G4
Moredun Park Way 51 G3
Moredunvale Bank 51 F2
Moredunvale Grn 51 F2
Moredunvale Gro 51 F2
Moredunvale Loan 51 F2
Moredunvale Park 51 F3
Moredunvale Pl 51 G2
Moredunvale Rd 51 F3
Moredunvale View 51 F2
Moredunvale Way 51 F2

Morningside Ct 38 D6
Morningside Dri 38 C6
Morningside Gdns 38 B6
Morningside Gro 38 C6
Morningside Park 38 D4
Morningside Pl 38 D4
Morningside Rd 38 D2
Morningside Ter 38 D5
Morrison St 24 D5
Morrison St La 4 A5
Morrisons Clo 5 E3
Morton St 29 E5
Mortonhall Gate 50 A6
Mortonhall Park Av 50 C6
Mortonhall Park Bank 50 C6
Mortonhall Park Cres 50 B6
Mortonhall Park Dri 50 B6
Mortonhall Park Gdns 50 B6
Mortonhall Park Grn 50 B6
Mortonhall Park Gro 50 B6
Mortonhall Park Loan 50 B6
Mortonhall Park Pl 50 C6
Mortonhall Park Ter 50 C6
Mortonhall Park View 50 B6
Mortonhall Park Way 50 B6
Mortonhall Rd 39 G5
Morven St 21 H3
Mossgift Walk 50 C1
Moston Ter 40 B3
Mound Pl 4 C3
Mount Lodge Pl 28 C4
Mount Vernon Rd 50 D2
Mountbarns Gdns 50 D2
Mountcastle 27 G4
Mountcastle Bank 28 A4
Mountcastle Cres 27 G4
Mountcastle Dri Nth 27 G4
Mountcastle Dri Sth 28 A5
Mountcastle Gdns 27 H4
Mountcastle Grn 27 G3
Mountcastle Loan 27 H4
Mountcastle Park 27 H3
Mountcastle Pl 27 G3
Mountcastle Ter 27 G4
Mounthooly Loan 49 F5
Mucklets Rd 43 H4
Muir Wood Cres 45 G5
Muir Wood Dri 45 G6
Muir Wood Gro 45 G6
Muir Wood Pl 45 G5
Muir Wood Rd 45 F6
Muirdale Ter 23 F2
Muirend Av 46 C4
Muirhouse Av 13 F5
Muirhouse Bank 13 E5
Muirhouse Cres 13 F4
Muirhouse Dri 13 E4
Muirhouse Gdns 12 D4
Muirhouse Gro 12 D4
Muirhouse Loan 13 E5
Muirhouse Medway 13 E5
Muirhouse Park 13 E5
Muirhouse Parkway 13 E4
Muirhouse Pl East 13 F5
Muirhouse Pl West 13 E5
Muirhouse Ter 13 E5
Muirhouse View 13 E4
Muirhouse Way 13 E4
Mulberry Pl 15 H4
Munro Dri 46 D6
Munro Pl 25 F1
Murano Pl 26 A1
Murdoch Ter 38 C1
Murieston Cres 38 B1
Murieston Cres La 38 B1
Murieston La 38 B1
Murieston P l 38 B1
Murieston Rd 38 B1
Murieston Ter 38 B1
Murray Cotts 35 H1
Murray Pl 22 B6
Murrayburn App 46 A1
Murrayburn Dri 46 A1
Murrayburn Gate 46 A1
Murrayburn Gdns 36 B6
Murrayburn Grn 46 B1
Murrayburn Gro 46 B1
Murrayburn Park 46 B1
Murrayburn Pl 46 B1
Murrayburn Rd 46 A1
Murrayfield Av 23 H5
Murrayfield Dri 23 G5
Murrayfield Gdns 23 H5
Murrayfield Pl 23 H5
Murrayfield Rd 23 H4
Musselburgh By-Pass 43 E2
Musselburgh Rd 29 E5
Myreside Ct 38 B5
Myreside Mews 38 B5

Myreside Rd 38 B5
Myrtle Ter 38 B2
Nantwich Dri 17 H6
Napier Rd 38 C2
Nellfield 50 D2
Nelson Pl 25 F2
Nelson St 25 F2
Nether Craigour 51 G1
Nether Craigwell 5 G2
Nether Currie Cres 45 F5
Nether Currie Pl 45 F5
Nether Currie Rd 45 G5
Netherbank 50 B5
Netherby Rd 14 D3
New Arthur Pl 5 F5
New Belfield 27 G5
New Broompark 1 F2
New Johns Pl 5 F6
New Kirkgate 16 B4
New La 15 G2
New Liston Rd 6 A4
New Market Rd 37 F5
New Orchardfield 16 A5
*New Orchardfield La, Orchardfield La 16 A5
New Skinners Clo 5 E3
New St 5 F1
New Tower Pl 28 C3
Newbattle Ter 39 E4
Newbridge Rd 9 D6
Newcraighall 42 C3
Newcraighall Dri 43 F3
Newcraighall Rd 43 E3
Newhaven Pl 15 G2
Newhaven Rd 15 G2
Newington Rd 40 A2
Newlands Park 40 B3
Newmains Rd 8 D2
Newmills Av 54 C2
Newmills Cres 54 C3
Newmills Gro 54 C2
Newmills Rd 54 C2
Newtoft St 51 G5
Newton Church Rd 52 C3
Newton St 38 A2
Nicolson Sq 5 E5
Nicolson St 5 E5
Niddrie Cotts 42 D3
Niddrie Farm Gro 41 G3
Niddrie House Av 42 A4
Niddrie House Gdns 42 B4
Niddrie House Gro 42 A4
Niddrie House Park 42 A4
Niddrie House Sq 42 A4
Niddrie Mains Ct 42 A3
Niddrie Mains Dri 41 G3
Niddrie Mains Rd 41 G3
Niddrie Mains Ter 41 G2
Niddrie Marischal Cres 42 A3
Niddrie Marischal Dri 42 A4
Niddrie Marischal Gdns 42 A3
Niddrie Marischal Grn 42 A4
Niddrie Marischal Gro 42 A3
Niddrie Marischal Loan 42 A3
Niddrie Marischal Pl 42 A4
Niddrie Marischal Rd 42 A4
Niddrie Marischal St 42 A3
Niddrie Mill Av 42 B2
Niddrie Mill Cres 42 B2
Niddrie Mill Gro 42 B3
Niddrie Mill Pl 42 B2
Niddrie Mill Ter 42 B3
Niddry St 5 E3
Niddry St Sth 5 E4
Nigel Loan 50 D2
Nile Gro 39 E5
Ninians Row 16 D6
Nisbet Pl 16 D6
Noble Pl 16 D5
North Bank St 4 C3
North Bridge 5 E2
North Bridge Arcade 5 E3
North Bughtlin Bank 21 F3
North Bughtlin Brae 21 F3
North Bughtlin Field 21 F2
North Bughtlin Gate 21 F3
North Bughtlin Neuk 21 F3
North Bughtlin Pl 21 G3
North Bughtlin Rigg 21 F3
North Bughtlin Road 21 F3
North Bughtlin Side 21 F2
North Cairntow 41 F2
North Charlotte St 4 A2
North East Circus Pl 25 E2
North East
Cumberland St La 25 F2
North Fort St 15 H2

North Grays Clo 5 E3
North Greens 42 C2
North Gyle Av 21 F6
North Gyle Dri 21 F6
North Gyle Farm Ct 21 F6
North Gyle Farm La 21 F6
North Gyle Gro 21 E6
North Gyle Loan 21 F6
North Gyle Park 21 F6
North Gyle Rd 21 G5
North Gyle Ter 21 E6
North Hillhousefield 15 H2
North Junction St 16 A3
North Leith Sands 16 A2
North Meadow Walk 4 C6
North Meggetland 38 A4
North Park Ter 24 C1
North Peffer Pl 41 G2
North St 32 B6
North St Andrew St 4 D1
North St Andrew St La 4 D1
North St David St 4 C1
North Werber Park 14 A6
North West Circus Pl 25 E2
North West
Cumberland St La 25 F2
Northcote St 24 B6
Northfield Av 27 F4
Northfield Broadway 27 G3
Northfield Circus 27 G4
Northfield Cres 27 G4
Northfield Dri 27 G5
Northfield Farm Av 27 G5
Northfield Farm Rd 27 G4
Northfield Gdns 27 G5
Northfield Gro 27 H5
Northfield Park 27 H4
Northfield Park Gro 27 H4
Northfield Rd 27 F4
Northfield Sq 27 G4
Northfield Ter 27 G4
Northlawn Ct 12 B5
Northlawn Ter 12 B5
Northumberland Pl 25 G2
Northumberland Pl Lane 25 G2
Northumberland St 4 B1
Northumberland St
Nth East 25 F2
Northumberland St
Nth West La 25 F2
Northumberland St
Sth East La 25 F2
Northumberland St
Sth West La 4 B1
Northview Ct 13 F4
Norton Park 26 C2
Nottingham Pl 5 E1
Oak La 22 B3
Oak Pl 5 F5
Oakville Ter 16 D6
Observatory Grn 39 H5
Observatory Rd 39 H5
Ochiltree Gdns 51 E1
Ogilvie Ter 38 B3
Old Assembly Clo 5 E3
Old Broughton 25 G2
Old Burdiehouse Rd 53 B2
Old Church La 41 E1
Old Dalkeith Rd, Danderhall 52 A2
Old Dalkeith Rd, Nether Liberton 40 D4
Old Farm Av 47 F4
Old Fishmarket Clo 4 D4
Old Hay Weight 25 F5
Old Kirk Rd 22 B5
Old Liston Rd 9 D6
Old Mill La 40 C6
Old Newmills Rd 54 C2
Old Playhouse Clo 5 F3
*Old Stamp Office Clo, High St 5 E3
Old Tolbooth Wynd 5 F2
Orchard Bank 24 A2
Orchard Brae 24 B2
Orchard Brae Av 24 B2
Orchard Brae Gdns 24 B2
Orchard Brae Gdns West 24 B2
Orchard Brae Way 24 B2
Orchard Cres 24 A3
Orchard Dri 24 A3
Orchard Gro 24 B2
Orchard Pl 24 B2
Orchard Rd 24 A3
Orchard Rd Loan 50 C2
Orchard Rd Sth 24 A3
Orchard Ter 24 A2
Orchard Toll 24 A3
Orchardfield Av 36 B1

Orchardfield La 16 A5
Orchardhead Rd 50 C1
Ormelie Ter 29 E5
Ormidale Ter 23 G5
Ormiston Ter 22 B6
Orrok Park 40 C6
Orrvale 54 C4
Orwell Pl 24 C6
Orwell Ter 24 C6
Osborne Ter 24 B5
Oswald Ct 39 G4
Oswald Rd 39 G4
Oswald Ter 36 A1
Otterburn Park 47 F1
Oxcars Ct 12 D4
Oxcraig St 14 B1
Oxford St 40 A1
Oxford Ter 24 D3
Oxgangs Av 48 B4
Oxgangs Bank 48 B5
Oxgangs Brae 48 C5
Oxgangs Broadway 48 B5
Oxgangs Cres 48 B3
Oxgangs Dri 48 B3
Oxgangs Farm Av 48 A5
Oxgangs Farm Dri 48 A5
Oxgangs Farm Gdns 48 B5
Oxgangs Farm Gro 48 A4
Oxgangs Farm Loan 48 B5
Oxgangs Farm Ter 48 B4
Oxgangs Gdns 48 B4
Oxgangs Grn 48 C4
Oxgangs Gro 48 B3
Oxgangs Hill 48 C4
Oxgangs Ho 48 B4
Oxgangs Loan 48 C3
Oxgangs Medway 48 C5
Oxgangs Park 48 B4
Oxgangs Path 48 B5
Oxgangs Pl 48 B4
Oxgangs Rise 48 B4
Oxgangs Road 48 C5
Oxgangs Road Nth 48 A2
Oxgangs Row 48 B4
Oxgangs St 48 B4
Oxgangs Ter 48 A4
Oxgangs View 48 C5

Paisley Av 27 F4
Paisley Clo 5 E3
Paisley Cres 27 E4
Paisley Dri 27 F5
Paisley Gro 27 F5
Paisley Ter 27 F4
Palmer Pl 55 E1
Palmer Rd 55 E1
Palmerston Pl 24 C4
Palmerston Rd 39 G2
Panmure Clo 5 G3
Panmure Pl 4 B6
Papes Cotts 24 A5
Park Av 28 B5
Park Cres 50 D2
Park Gdns 50 D2
Park Gro 50 D3
Park La 28 B6
Park Pl 15 G2
Park Rd 15 F2
Park Ter 43 F3
Park View 43 F3
Parker Av 27 H3
Parker Rd 27 H3
Parker Ter 27 H3
Parkgrove Av 21 H1
Parkgrove Bank 21 H2
Parkgrove Cres 21 H2
Parkgrove Dri 21 G1
Parkgrove Gdns 21 G2
Parkgrove Grn 21 H2
Parkgrove Loan 21 G1
Parkgrove Neuk 21 H2
Parkgrove Path 22 A2
Parkgrove Pl 22 A1
Parkgrove Rd 21 H1
Parkgrove Row 21 H2
Parkgrove St 22 A1
Parkgrove Ter 21 H2
Parkgrove View 21 H2
Parkhead Av 36 B6
Parkhead Cres 36 C6
Parkhead Dri 36 B6
Parkhead Gdns 36 C5
Parkhead Gro 36 C5
Parkhead Loan 36 C5
Parkhead Pl 36 C5
Parkhead St 36 B5
Parkhead Ter 36 C5
Parkhead View 36 B6
Parkside 9 C6
Parkside St 40 A1

Parkside Ter 40 B1
Parkview Pl 16 D5
*Parliament Sq,
　Main St 15 G2
Parliament Sq 4 D4
Parliament St 16 B3
Parrotshot 42 C2
Parsons Green Ter 27 E3
Path Brae 8 D3
Paties Rd 47 F2
Pattison St 16 C4
Peacocktail Clo 42 C3
Pearce Av 21 H5
Pearce Gro 21 H5
Pearce Rd 21 H5
Peatville Gdns 46 D1
Peatville Ter 36 D6
Peel Ter 40 B3
Peffer Bank 41 F3
Peffer Pl 41 F3
Peffer St 41 F3
Peffermill Ct 41 F4
Peffermill Rd 40 D4
Peggys Mill Rd 11 F4
Pembroke Pl 24 B6
Pennywell Cotts 13 F3
Pennywell Ct 13 F4
Pennywell Gdns 13 E4
Pennywell Gro 13 E4
Pennywell Medway 13 E3
Pennywell Pl 13 F3
Pennywell Rd 13 F3
Pennywell Villas 13 F3
Pentland Av, Colinton 46 D4
Pentland Av, Currie 55 E2
Pentland Cres 48 D3
Pentland Dri 48 C4
Pentland Gdns 48 C3
Pentland Gro 48 D3
Pentland Howe 55 F2
Pentland Pl 55 F2
Pentland Rd 46 D4
Pentland Ter 48 D3
Pentland Ter 48 D3
Pentland View, Currie 55 E2
Pentland View,
　Fairmilehead 48 C4
Pentland View Ct 55 F2
Pentland View Rd 8 C2
Perth St 25 F1
Peveril Ter 50 C2
Picardy Pl 25 H2
Pier Pl 15 F2
Piersfield Gro 27 F3
Piersfield Pl 27 G3
Piersfield Ter 27 F3
Piershill La 27 F3
Piershill Pl 27 F3
Piershill Sq East 27 F3
Piershill Sq West 27 F3
Piershill Ter 27 F3
Pilrig Cotts 16 A6
Pilrig Gdns 15 H6
Pilrig St 16 A5
Pilton Av 14 A4
Pilton Cres 14 B3
Pilton Dri 14 B3
Pilton Dri Nth 14 B2
Pilton Gdns 14 B3
Pilton Loan 14 B3
Pilton Park 14 B3
Pilton Pl 14 A3
Pipe La 28 B3
Pipe St 28 B3
Pirniefield Bank 17 E5
Pirniefield Gdns 17 E5
Pirniefield Grò 17 E5
Pirniefield Ter 17 E5
Pirrie St 16 B4
Pitlochry Pl 26 C2
Pitsligo Rd 39 E3
Pitt St 15 H4
Pitville St 28 D4
Pitville St La 28 D4
Playfair Steps 4 C3
Pleasance 5 F4
Plewlands Av 38 C6
Plewlands Gdns 38 C5
Plewlands Ter C6
Pleydell Pl 50 D2
Pollocks Clo 4 D4
Polwarth Cres 38 C2
Polwarth Gdns 38 C2
Polwarth Gro 38 C2
Polwarth Park 38 C2
Polwarth Pl 38 C2
Polwarth Ter 38 B4
Ponton St 4 A6
Poplar La 16 C4
Porland Ter 16 A3

Porterfield Rd 24 A1
Portgower Pl 24 D2
Portland St 15 H3
Portobello High St 28 B3
Portobello Rd 27 F3
Portsburgh Sq 4 B5
Potterrow 5 E5
Potterrow Port 5 E5
Prestonfield Av 40 C3
Prestonfield Cres 40 C4
Prestonfield Gdns 40 C3
Prestonfield Rd 40 C3
Prestonfield Ter 40 C3
Priestfield Av 40 D3
Priestfield Cres 40 D3
Priestfield Gdns 40 D3
Priestfield Gro 40 D2
Priestfield Rd 40 C2
Priestfield Rd Nth 40 C2
Primrose Bank Rd 15 E2
Primrose Dri 10 B6
Primrose St 16 C5
Primrose Ter 38 B2
Prince Regent St 16 A3
Princes St 4 A3
Promenade 28 A1
Promenade Ter 28 B2
Prospect Bank 25 F1
Prospect Bank Gdns 16 D6
Prospect Bank Gro 17 E5
Prospect Bank Pl 17 E5
Prospect Bank Rd 16 D5
Prospect Bank Ter 17 E5
Quality St 12 C6
Quality St La 12 C6
Quarry Clo 5 F6
Quarry Cotts 42 C3
Quarry Howe 54 B4
Quayside St 16 B3
Queen Anne Dri 9 E6
Queen Charlotte La 16 C4
Queen Charlotte St 16 C4
Queen St 4 A2
Queen St Gdns East 4 C1
Queen St Gdns West 4 B1
Queens Av 23 F2
Queens Av Sth 23 G2
Queens Bay Cres 29 E6
Queens Cres 40 B3
Queens Dri 5 G5
Queens Gdns 23 G1
Queens Park Av 26 D3
Queens Park Ct 27 E3
Queens Rd 23 G2
Queens Walk 41 H4
Queensferry Rd,
　Barnton 21 E1
Queensferry Rd, Dean 24 A3
Queensferry Rd,
　Kirkliston 8 D1
Queensferry St 24 D4
Queensferry St Lane 24 D4
Queensferry Ter 24 B3
Quilts Wynd 16 A4
Radical Rd 5 H5
Raeburn Mews 24 D2
Raeburn Pl 24 D2
Raeburn St 24 D2
Ramsay Gdns 4 C4
Ramsay La 4 C4
Ramsay Pl 28 C3
Randolph Cres 24 D4
Randolph La 25 E4
Randolph Pl 25 E4
Rankeillor St 5 F6
Rankin Av 40 A5
Rankin Dri 40 A5
Rankin Rd 40 A5
Rannoch Gro 22 B3
Rannoch Pl 22 B3
Rannoch Rd 22 A3
Rannoch Ter 22 A3
Ransome Gdns 22 A3
Ratcliff Ter 40 A3
Rathbone Pl 28 C3
Ratho Park Rd 32 C5
Ravelrig Hill 54 A4
Ravelrig Park 54 A4
Ravelrig Rd 54 A1
Ravelston Dykes 23 F4
Ravelston Dykes La 23 E4
Ravelston Dykes Rd 23 E3
Ravelston Gdn 23 G4
Ravelston Heights 23 G3
Ravelston Ho Gro 23 G3
Ravelston Ho Loan 23 G3
Ravelston Ho Park 23 G3

Ravelston Ho Rd 23 G3
Ravelston Park 24 B4
Ravelston Pl 24 B3
Ravelston Rise 23 G4
Ravelston Ter 24 B3
Ravenscroft Gdns 51 G5
Ravenscroft Pl 51 G5
Ravenscroft St 51 G5
Ravenswood Av 50 D1
Redbraes Gro 15 H5
Redbraes Pl 15 H5
Redcroft St 52 B2
Redford Av 47 H4
Redford Bank 47 G4
Redford Cres 47 F5
Redford Dri 47 F5
Redford Gdns 47 G4
Redford Gro 47 H4
Redford Loan 47 F5
Redford Neuk 47 H4
Redford Pl 47 H4
Redford Rd 47 F4
Redford Ter 47 G5
Redford Walk 47 H4
Redgauntlet Ter 51 E1
Redhall Av 37 E6
Redhall Bank Rd 47 E1
Redhall Cres 37 E5
Redhall Dri 37 E6
Redhall Gdns 37 E5
Redhall Gro 37 E6
Redhall House Dri 47 F1
Redhall Pl 37 E6
Redhall View 37 F6
Redheughs Av 35 F3
Redheughs Muir 35 F3
Redheughs Rigg 35 F2
Reford Pl 47 H4
Regent Pl 26 C2
Regent Rd 5 F2
Regent St 28 C4
Regent St La 28 C3
Regent Ter 5 G2
Regent Ter Mews 5 H1
Regents Gate 40 B1
Regis Ct 11 F5
Register Pl 4 D2
Reid Ter 24 D1
Reids Clo 5 G3
Reids Ct 5 G3
Relugas Gdns 40 A4
Relugas Pl 39 H4
Relugas Rd 39 H4
Research Av One 45 E2
Research Av Two 45 E2
Research Park Rd 45 E3
Restalrig Av 27 E2
Restalrig Circus 17 E6
Restalrig Cres 17 E6
Restalrig Dri 27 E2
Restalrig Gdns 27 E1
Restalrig Ho 27 E1
Restalrig Park 16 D6
Restalrig Rd 16 D5
Restalrig Rd Sth 27 E2
Restalrig Sq 27 E1
Restalrig Ter 16 C5
Riccarton Av 55 F1
Riccarton Cres 55 F1
Riccarton Dri 55 F1
Riccarton Gro 55 F1
Riccarton Mains Rd 45 E1
Richmond Gdns 51 E1
Richmond La 5 F5
Richmond Pl 5 F5
Richmond Ter 24 C6
Riddles Ct 4 D4
Riding Park 11 F5
Rillbank Cres 39 G1
Rillbank Ter 39 G1
Ringwood Pl 50 D1
Rintoul Pl 25 E1
Riselaw Cres 48 D3
Riselaw Pl 48 D2
Riselaw Rd 48 D2
Riselaw Ter 48 D2
Ritchie Pl 38 B2
Riverside Cres 23 G6
Riverside Gro 23 G6
Riverside Rd 23 F6
Riverside 9 C6
Riverside Rd 10 C5
Robbs Loan 37 G3
Robbs Loan Gro 37 G3
Robert Burns Dri 50 C1
Robertson Av 38 A2
Robertsons Clo 5 E4
Robertsons Ct 5 H2
Rocheid Pk 14 B5

Rochester Ter
Roddinglaw Rd
Rodney St
Ronaldsons Wharf
Rose Ct
Rose Park
Rose St
Rose St North La
Rose St South La 50 D1
Rosebank Cotts
Rosebank Gdns
Rosebank Gro
Rosebank Rd
Rosebery Cres
Rosebery Cres La
Roseburn Av
Roseburn Cliff
Roseburn Cres
Roseburn Dri
Roseburn Gdns
Roseburn Pl
Roseburn St
Roseburn Ter
Rosefield Av
Rosefield Av La
Rosefield La
Rosefield Pl
Rosefield St
Rosemount Bldgs
Roseneath Ter
Rosevale Pl
Rosevale Ter
Roseville Gdns
Ross Gdns
Ross Pl
Ross Rd
Rossie Pl
Rosslyn Cres
Rosslyn Ter
Rothesay Mews
Rothesay Pl
Rothesay Ter
Roull Gro
Roull Pl
Roull Rd
Rowan Tree Av
Rowan Tree Gro
Rowan Tree Pl
Roxburgh Pl
Roxburgh St
Royal Circus
Royal Cres
Royal Mile
Royal Park Pl
Royal Park Ter
Royal Ter
Royston Mains Av
Royston Mains Cres
Royston Mains Gdns
Royston Mains Grn
Royston Mains Pl
Royston Mains Rd
Royston Mains St
Royston Ter
Russell Pl
Russell Rd
Rustic Cotts
Rutherford Dri
Rutland Ct
Rutland Sq
Rutland St
Ryehill Av
Ryehill Gdns
Ryehill Pl
Ryehill Ter

Saddletree Loan 4 D4
St Albans Rd 11 F5
St Andrew Pl 39 G1
St Andrew Sq 39 G1
St Anthonys Pl 50 D1
St Anthonys St 25 E1
St Bernards Cres 48 D3
St Bernards Bri 48 D2
St Bernards Row 48 D2
St Catherines Gdns
St Catherines Pl 38 B2
St Clair Av 23 G6
St Clair Pl 23 G6
St Clair Rd 23 F6
St Clair St 9 C6
St Clair Ter 10 C5
St Colme St 37 G3
St Davids Pl 37 G3
St Davids Ter 50 C1
St Fillans Ter 38 A2
St James Pl 5 E4
St James Sq 5 H2
St John St 14 B5

Name	Ref	Name	Ref
Av	22 C6	Seafield Rd East	17 G5
Cres	22 C6	Seafield St	17 F5
Gdns	22 C6	Seafield Ter	17 E5
Hill	5 F4	Seafield Way	17 H6
Pl	16 C4	Seaforth Dri	23 F2
Rd	22 A6	Sealcarr St	14 A1
Ter	22 C6	Seaport St	16 C3
ines Brae	50 C4	Seaview Cres	29 F5
ines Cres	50 C5	Seaview Ter	29 F5
ines Loan	50 D5	Second Gait	44 D2
ds Bank	5 G6	Semple St	4 A5
ds Cragg	5 G6	Seton Pl	39 H2
ds Hill	5 G6	Shaftesbury Park	38 A3
ds La	5 G6	Shandon Cres	38 A3
ds St	5 F6	Shandon Pl	38 A3
ets Rd	39 E3	Shandon Rd	38 A3
La	28 C4	Shandon St	38 A3
Pl	28 C4	Shandon Ter	38 A3
Pl	28 D5	Shanter Way	50 C1
Pl Lane	28 D4	Shanwick Pl	25 E4
St	5 F3	Sharpdale Loan	40 C5
s Dri	22 A6	Shawfair Rd	52 D1
s Rd	22 A6	Shaws Pl	16 A6
s Ter	38 C6	Shaws Ter	16 A6
Sq	5 F6	Sheriff Brae	16 B3
St	5 F6	Sherrif Park	16 B3
Bldgs	38 D1	Shore	16 B3
Pl	38 D1	Shore Pl	16 B3
s Ter	38 C6	Shrub Mount	28 B3
ns Pl	25 E2	Shrub Pl	26 A1
ns St	25 E2	Shrub Place La	26 A1
Pl	38 C3	Sienna Gdns	39 H2
s Rd	39 H4	Sighthill Av	36 B6
St	25 F2	Sighthill Bank	36 A5
ier Pl	16 D4	Sighthill Ct	36 A5
ier St	16 C3	Sighthill Cres	36 A6
Pl	40 A2	Sighthill Dri	46 A1
Rd	40 A2	Sighthill Gdns	36 B6
Pl	26 C2	Sighthill Grn	36 A5
	4 A4	Sighthill Gro	36 B6
Ter	13 F3	Sighthill Loan	36 A6
Cres	13 E3	Sighthill Neuk	36 A6
Gdns	13 E3	Sighthill Park	36 B6
Gro	13 E3	Sighthill Pl	36 A6
	16 B3	Sighthill Rise	46 A1
Gdns	28 B4	Sighthill Rd	36 A6
Pl	16 B3	Sighthill St	36 A6
St	16 B3	Sighthill Ter	36 A6
ink	24 B6	Sighthill View	36 A6
Av	37 G2	Sighthill Wynd	36 B5
Cres	23 E6	Silverknowes Av	12 C5
Gdns	23 F6	Silverknowes Bank	12 D5
Gro	23 F6	Silverknowes Brae	12 D5
Hall Gdns	23 G6	Silverknowes Ct	12 D4
Loan	23 F6	Silverknowes Cres	12 C5
Mains Av	36 D3	Silverknowes Dell	12 D6
Mains Bank	36 D3	Silverknowes Dri	12 C5
Mains Dri	36 C4	Silverknowes Eastway	12 D4
Mains Gdns	36 C4	Silverknowes Gdns	12 D4
Mains Gro	36 D4	Silverknowes Grn	12 D5
Mains Loan	36 C3	Silverknowes Gro	12 D4
Mains Park	36 C3	Silverknowes Hill	12 C5
Mains Pl	36 C4	Silverknowes Loan	12 C5
Mains St	36 C3	Silverknowes Midway	12 D5
Mains Ter	36 C3	Silverknowes Neuk	13 E6
Park	23 F6	Silverknowes Parkway	12 D4
Rd	36 B1	Silverknowes Pl	12 D4
Rd Nth	36 B1	Silverknowes Rd	12 C2
Av	37 F1	Silverknowes Rd East	12 D5
all Av West	37 F1	Silverknowes Rd Sth	12 D6
Circus	23 F6	Silverknowes Southway	13 E5
Cres	23 F6	Silverknowes Ter	12 C5
Dri	23 F6	Silverknowes View	12 D5
Gro	23 F6	Simon Sq	5 E4
Pl	23 F6	Sir Harry Lauder Rd	28 A3
Ter	23 F6	Sir William	
St	25 E2	Fraser Homes	47 E3
	40 A4	Slaeside	54 B4
	40 B4	Slateford Rd	37 G5
	40 B4	Sleigh Dri	26 D1
rg Pl	25 E1	Sleigh Gdns	27 E1
rg St	25 E1	Sloan St	16 B6
urg Ter,		Smithfield St	38 A2
urg St	25 E1	Smiths Pl	16 B5
e Row	11 G3	Smithy Green Av	52 C3
use Pl	40 A2	Somerset Pl	16 C5
nd	32 B5	South Barnton Av	12 B6
	39 H1	South Beechwood	23 E6
Hill Pl,	39 H2	South Bridge	5 E3
s Gdns	39 H2	South Charlotte St	4 A3
ill Rd	39 G2	South Clerk St	5 E5
s	27 E3	South College St	5 E5
	25 G1	South East Circus Pl	25 E2
Bldgs	5 E3	South East	
	17 F5	Cumberland St La	25 F2
	17 E5	South Ettrick Rd	38 C3
	17 E5	South Fort St	15 H5
	17 E4	South Gillsland Rd	38 C4
		South Gray St	40 A3
		South Grays Clo	5 E3

Name	Ref	Name	Ref
South Groathill Av	23 G2	Steels Pl	39 E4
South Gyle Access	35 H3	Stenhouse Av	37 E2
South Gyle Broadway	34 D1	Stenhouse Av West	36 D3
South Gyle Cres	35 F2	Stenhouse Cotts	37 E4
South Gyle Cres La	35 G3	Stenhouse Cres	37 E4
South Gyle Gdns	35 G1	Stenhouse Dri	36 C3
South Gyle Loan	35 G2	Stenhouse Gdns	37 E3
South Gyle Mains	35 G2	Stenhouse Gdns Nth	36 D3
South Gyle Park	35 G2	Stenhouse Gro	37 E3
South Gyle Wynd	35 H2	Stenhouse Mill Cres	37 E4
South Lauder Rd	39 H3	Stenhouse Mill La	37 E4
South Learmonth Av	24 C2	Stenhouse Mill Wynd	37 F4
South Learmonth Gdns	24 C2	Stenhouse Pl East	37 E3
South Lorne Pl	16 B6	Stenhouse Pl West	37 E3
South Maybury	21 E6	Stenhouse Rd	37 E4
South Mellis Park	27 G3	Stenhouse St East	37 E3
South Morton St	29 E5	Stenhouse St West	36 C4
South Oswald Rd	39 F4	Stenhouse Ter	37 E3
South Oxford St	40 A1	Stennis Gdns	51 E3
South Park	15 G2	Stevenlaws Clo	5 E3
South Sloan St	26 B1	Stevenson Av	37 G2
South St Andrew St	4 D2	Stevenson Dri	37 E3
South St Davids St	4 D2	Stevenson Gro	37 G2
South Trinity Rd	15 E3	Stevenson Rd	37 G2
South West		Stevenson Ter	37 G2
Cumberland St La	25 F2	Stewart Av	54 D3
Southbank	12 B5	Stewart Cres	55 E2
Southbank Ct	12 B5	Stewart Field	15 H5
Southfield Bank	28 A6	Stewart Gdns	55 E2
Southfield Farm Gro	27 H5	Stewart Pl	8 D2
Southfield Gdns East	28 A6	Stewart Rd	55 E2
Southfield Gdns West	27 H6	Stewart Ter	38 A2
Southfield Loan	28 A6	Stirling Rd	15 E3
Southfield Pl	28 B5	Stoney Path	37 E6
Southfield Rd East	28 A6	Strachan Gdns	23 E2
Southfield Rd West	27 H6	Strachan Rd	23 E1
Southfield Sq	28 A6	Straiton Pl	28 C3
Southfield Ter	27 H6	Strathalmond Ct	21 E1
Southhouse Av	50 C6	Strathalmond Gro	21 E1
Southhouse Broadway	53 B2	Strathalmond Park	21 E1
Southhouse Cres	51 E6	Strathalmond Rd	20 D1
Southhouse Gro	53 B1	Strathearn Pl	39 E3
Southhouse Gro	50 D6	Strathearn Rd	39 F3
Southhouse Medway	50 D6	Strathfillan Rd	39 F3
Southhouse Paths	50 D6	Stratton Rd	53 A3
Southhouse Rd	53 B1	Stuart Cres	21 G4
Southhouse Sq	53 B1	Stuart Gro	21 G4
Southhouse Ter	51 E6	Stuart Park	21 F4
Southlawn Ct	12 B5	Stuart Sq	21 G4
Soutra Ct	50 D4	Stuart Wynd	21 G4
Spa Pl	28 C3	Succoth Av	23 H4
Speedwell Av	52 B2	Succoth Ct	23 H4
Spence St	40 B2	Succoth Gdns	23 G4
Spencer Pl	15 E3	Succoth Pl	23 H4
Spey St	16 A6	Suffolk Rd	40 B4
Spey St Mews	16 A6	Sugar House Clo	5 F3
Spiers Pl	16 B4	Summer Bank	25 G1
Spittal St	4 A5	Summer Pl	15 F6
Spittalfield Cres	5 F6	Summerfield Gdns	16 D5
Spottiswood Rd	39 F2	Summerfield Pl	16 D5
Spottiswood St	39 F1	Summerhall	40 A1
Spring Gdns	26 C3	Summerhall Sq	40 A1
Springfield	16 A5	Summerside Pl	15 G3
Springfield Bldgs	16 B5	Summerside St	15 H3
Springfield St	16 B5	Summertrees Ct	40 D6
Springvalley Gdns	38 D4	Sunbury Mews	24 C4
Springvalley Ter	38 D4	Sunbury Pl	24 C4
Springwell Pl	24 B6	Sunbury St	24 C4
Springwood Park	50 D2	Sunnybank	26 D3
Spylaw Av	46 D4	Sunnybank Pl	26 C3
Spylaw Bank Rd	46 D3	Surrey Pl	24 B6
Spylaw Park	46 D4	Sutherland St	24 B6
Spylaw Rd	38 B4	Swan Spring Av	48 C4
Spylaw St	47 E4	Swanfield	16 A4
Stable La	38 D4	Swanston Av	48 D6
Stafford St	24 D4	Swanston Cres	48 D6
Stair Park	23 G5	Swanston Dri	49 E6
Stanedykehead	50 B4	Swanston Gdns	48 D6
Stanhope Pl	24 B6	Swanston Grn	48 C6
Stanhope St	24 B5	Swanston Gro	49 E6
Stanley Pl	26 C3	Swanston Loan	48 D6
Stanley Rd	15 F3	Swanston Muir	48 C6
Stanley St	28 B5	Swanston Park	48 C6
Stanwell St	16 A5	Swanston Pl	48 D6
Stapley Av	27 G1	Swanston Rd	48 C6
Starbank Rd	15 F2	Swanston Row	48 D6
Starks Cotts	48 A3	Swanston Ter	48 D6
Station Brae	28 B5	Swanston View	48 D6
Station Loan	54 C3	Swanston Way	48 D6
Station Rd,		Sycamore Gdns	36 B1
Corstorphine	22 B6	Sycamore Ter	36 B1
Station Rd,		Sydney Park	27 H2
Kirkliston	8 D3	Sydney Pl	27 H2
Station Rd,		Sydney Ter	27 H2
Ratho Station	9 F6	Sylvan Pl	39 G1
Station Rd,		Talisman Pl	50 D1
Wester Hailes	46 A5	Tanfield La	25 F1
Station Ter	8 E2	Tantallon Pl	39 H2
Steads Pl	16 B5	Tarvit St	25 F6

Name	Ref
Tay St	38 C1
Taylor Gdns	16 A4
Taylor Pl	26 C3
Telfer Subway	24 C6
Telferton Causeway	28 A3
Telford Dri	13 H6
Telford Gdns	13 H6
Telford Pl	13 H6
Telford Rd	23 F1
Temple Park Cres	38 C2
Templeland Gro	22 A6
Templeland Rd	22 A5
Tennant St	16 A5
Teviot Pl	4 D5
Teviotdale Pl	25 E1
The Avenue	44 D3
The Bowling Grn	16 A4
The Causeway	41 E1
The Cedars	47 F3
The Circle	52 C2
The City of Edinburgh	
By-Pass	34 D1
The City of Edinburgh	
By-Pass, Wester Hailes	46 A2
The Crescent	38 D5
The East Way	27 G4
The Gallolee	47 H4
The Glebe, Kirkliston	8 D3
The Glebe, Cramond	11 G3
The Green, Balerno	54 D6
The Green,	
Silverknowes	12 D5
The Green Way	46 B1
The Jewel	42 C2
The Lade	54 D6
The Mound	4 C3
The Murrays	53 C1
The Murrays Brae	51 E6
The North Way	27 G4
The Northwalk	38 D5
The Paddockholm	36 C1
The Pillars	51 G3
The Pottery	28 C3
The Quilts	16 A4
The Spinney	51 G4
The Steils	48 B1
The Square, Danderhall	52 C2
The Square, Kirkliston	8 D3
The Tunnel	37 E6
The Wisp	42 C3
Third Gait	44 C3
Thirlestane La	39 F2
Thirlestane Rd	39 F2
Thistle Ct	4 C2
Thistle Pl	38 D1
Thistle St	4 B2
Thistle St La Nth East	4 C1
Thistle St La Nth West	4 C1
Thistle St La Sth East	4 C2
Thistle St La Sth West	4 B2
Thompson Cres	45 F6
Thompson Dri	45 G6
Thompson Gro	45 G6
Thompson Rd	55 G1
Thornburn Gro	47 G5
Thornburn Rd	47 F4
Thorntree Side	16 C6
Thorntree St	16 B5
Thornville Ter	16 C6
Thornybauk	4 A6
Threipmuir Av	54 C6
Threipmuir Cres	54 C6
Threipmuir Pl	54 C6
Timber Bush	16 C3
Tinto Pl	15 H5
Tipperlinn Rd	38 C3
Toddshill Rd	8 D3
Tolbooth Wynd,	
Canongate	5 F3
Tolbooth Wynd, Leith	16 B3
Tollcross	4 A6
Torduff Rd	46 D6
Torphichen Pl	24 D5
Torphichen St	24 D5
Torphin Rd	46 D5
Torrance Park	21 H3
Tower Pl	16 C3
Tower St	16 C3
Tower St Lane	16 C3
Trafalgar La	15 H4
Trafalgar St	15 H4
Traquair Park East	36 C1
Traquair Park West	36 B1
Trench Knowe	48 C6
Tresillian Gdns	50 D1
Trinity Ct	14 D4
Trinity Cres	15 E2
Trinity Gro	15 E3
Trinity Park Ho	15 E4
Trinity Rd	15 E3

Name	Ref
Tron Sq	5 E4
Trunks Clo	5 E3
Tryst Park	48 C6
Turner Av	54 B3
Turner Park	54 B3
Turnhouse Farm Rd	19 H3
Turnhouse Rd	19 F3
Tweeddale Ct	5 F3
Tylers Acre Av	36 B2
Tylers Acre Gdns	36 B2
Tylers Acre Rd	36 B1
Tynecastle La	38 B1
Ulster Cres	27 F4
Ulster Dri	27 F4
Ulster Gnds	27 G5
Ulster Gro	27 G5
Ulster Ter	27 F5
Union St	25 H2
Upper Bow	4 D4
Upper Coltbridge Ter	24 A5
Upper Craigour	51 G1
Upper Craigour Way	51 G1
Upper Cramond Ct	11 F5
Upper Dean Ter	24 D3
Upper Gilmore Pl	39 E1
Upper Gilmore Ter	39 E1
Upper Gray St	40 A2
Upper Grove Pl	24 D6
Vallences Entry	5 G3
Valleyfield St	39 E1
Vanburgh Pl	16 C5
Vandeleur Av	27 H2
Vandeleur Gro	27 H2
Vandeleur Pl	27 H2
*Veitchs Sq, Deanhaugh St	25 E2
Vennel	4 C5
Ventnor Ter	40 B3
Vexhim Park	42 C2
Victor Park Ter	22 A6
Victoria St	4 D4
Victoria Ter	4 C4
Viewcraig Gdns	5 F4
Viewcraig St	5 G4
Viewfield Rd	46 C4
Viewforth	38 D1
Viewforth Gdns	39 E2
Viewforth Sq	38 D1
Viewforth Ter	38 D1
Violet Ter	38 B2
Vivian Ter	12 D6
Waddell Pl	16 B5
Wains Pl	28 B3
Wakefield Av	28 A1
Walker St	24 D4
Walker Ter	24 D6
Walkers Ct	46 C1
Walkers Rig	46 B1
Walkers Wynd	46 C1
Walter Scott Av	40 D6
Wardie Av	14 D4
Wardie Cres	14 C3
Wardie Dell	14 C2
Wardie Field	14 C2
Wardie Gro	14 D2
Wardie House La	14 D2
Wardie Park	14 C4
Wardie Rd	14 D3
Wardie Sq	14 D2
Wardie Steps	14 D2
Wardieburn Dri	14 C2
Wardieburn Pl East	14 B2
Wardieburn Pl Nth	14 B2
Wardieburn Pl Sth	14 B3
Wardieburn Pl West	14 B2
Wardieburn Rd	14 B2
Wardieburn St East	14 B2
Wardieburn St West	14 B2
Wardieburn Ter	14 B3
Wardlaw Pl	38 A2
Wardlaw St	38 A2
Wardlaw Ter	38 A2
Wardrops Ct	4 D4
Warrender Park Cres	39 E2
Warrender Park Rd	39 E2
Warrender Park Ter	39 F1
Warriston Av	15 F5
Warriston Clo	4 D3
Warriston Cres	15 F6
Warriston Dri	15 E5
Warriston Farm Rd	44 A4
Warriston Gdns	15 E5
Warriston Gro	15 E5
Warriston Rd	15 E5
Warriston Ter	15 E5
Washington La	24 C6
Washington St	24 C6

Name	Ref
Water St	16 B4
Waterloo Pl	5 E2
Waters Clo	16 B3
Watertoun Rd	39 H5
Watson Cres	38 B2
Wauchope Av	41 H3
Wauchope Cres	41 H3
Wauchope Ho	42 A5
Wauchope Pl	41 H3
Wauchope Rd	42 A3
Wauchope Sq	42 A3
Wauchope Ter	41 H3
Waukmill Loan	54 D3
Waverley Bri	4 D2
Waverley Park	26 C3
Waverley Park Ter	26 C3
Waverley Pl	26 C2
Waverley Steps	4 D2
Weavers Knowe Cres	55 F1
Webster Steil	48 B1
*Websters Land, West Port	4 B5
Weir Ct	36 A5
Wellflats Rd	8 E2
Wellington Pl	16 C4
Wellington St	26 B2
Wemyss Pl	4 A1
Wemyss Pl Mews	4 A2
West Adam St	5 F5
West Annandale St	25 G1
West Approach Rd	24 C6
West Bow	4 C4
West Bowling Green St	15 H4
West Brighton Cres	28 B4
West Bryson Rd	38 B2
West Caiystane Rd	48 D5
West Carnethy Av	46 D5
West Castle Rd	38 C2
West Catherine Pl	24 B6
West Coates	24 B5
West College St	5 E4
West Ct, Craigmillar	41 H4
West Ct, Ravelston	23 G3
West Craigs Av	21 E6
West Craigs Cres	21 E6
West Croft	32 C5
West Cromwell St	16 A3
West Crosscauseway	5 E6
West End	4 A3
West Ferryfield	14 C4
West Fountain Pl	38 C1
West Granton Cres	13 F3
West Granton Dri	13 G3
West Granton Grn	13 F3
West Granton Pl	13 F3
West Granton Rd	13 F3
West Granton Row	13 G3
West Granton Ter	13 G3
West Mains Rd	40 A5
West Maitland St	24 D5
West Mayfield	40 A3
West Mill Rd	46 C4
West Montgomery Pl	26 A2
West Newington Pl	40 A2
West Nicolson St	5 E6
West Norton Pl	26 B2
West Park Pl	24 C6
West Pier	14 A1
West Pilton Av	13 G5
West Pilton Bank	13 F4
West Pilton Cres	13 F3
West Pilton Crossway	13 G4
West Pilton Dri	13 G3
West Pilton Gdns	13 G4
West Pilton Grn	13 G3
West Pilton Gro	13 G4
West Pilton Lea	13 G4
West Pilton Loan	13 G4
West Pilton Park	13 G4
West Pilton Pl	13 H4
West Pilton Rise	13 G4
West Pilton Road	13 H3
West Pilton St	13 G3
West Pilton Ter	13 G3
West Pilton View	13 F4
West Port	4 B5
West Preston St	40 A1
West Register St	4 D2
West Relugas Rd	39 H4
West Richmond St	5 F5
West Savile Rd	40 B4
West Savile Ter	39 H4
West Shore Rd	13 F2
West Silvermills La	25 E2
West Telferton	28 A3
West Tollcross	4 A6
West Werberside	14 B5
West Winnelstrae	14 B5
West Woods	14 A6
Westbank	12 B5

Name	Ref
Westbank La	28 B2
Westbank Pl	28 B2
Westbank St	28 B3
Westburn Av	45 H2
Westburn Gdns	45 H2
Westburn Gro	45 H2
Westburn Middlefield	45 H2
Westburn Park	46 A2
Westend Pl	24 C6
Wester Broom Av	35 H2
Wester Broom Dri	35 G2
Wester Broom Gdns	35 H1
Wester Broom Gro	35 H1
Wester Broom Pl	35 H1
Wester Broom Ter	35 H1
Wester Coates Av	24 A5
Wester Coates Gdns	24 A5
Wester Coates Pl	24 B5
Wester Coates Rd	24 B5
Wester Coates Ter	24 B5
*Wester Clo, Main St	15 G2
Wester Drylaw Av	13 F6
Wester Drylaw Dri	13 E6
Wester Drylaw Park	13 F6
Wester Drylaw Pl	13 E6
Wester Drylaw Row	23 G1
Wester Hailes Dri	46 A2
Wester Hailes Park	46 B1
Wester Hailes Rd	46 A1
Western Gdns	23 G6
Western Pl	23 F6
Western Ter	23 G6
Westfield Av	37 G1
Westfield Ct	37 G2
Westfield Rd	37 H1
Westfield St	37 H2
Westgarth Av	47 F4
Westhall Gdns	39 E2
Westland Cotts	51 G6
*Westmost Clo, Main St	15 G2
Wheatfield Pl	38 A1
Wheatfield Rd	38 A2
Wheatfield St	38 A1
Wheatfield Ter	38 A2
White Horse Clo	5 G2
White Park	38 A2
Whitedales	49 F5
Whitehall Ct	23 F1
Whitehall Rd	42 D3
Whitehill St	43 F3
Whitehouse Loan	39 E1
Whitehouse Rd	11 F4
Whitehouse Ter, Corstorphine	22 B6
Whitehouse Ter, Grange	39 F3
Whitelea Cres	54 B6
Whitelea Rd	54 B6
Whitson Cres	37 F2
Whitson Gro	37 E2
Whitson Pl East	37 F2
Whitson Pl West	37 F2
Whitson Rd	37 E2
Whitson Ter	37 F2
Whitson Walk	37 E2
Whitson Way	37 F2
Whyte Pl	26 C3
Wilfred Ter	27 E3
Wilkieston Rd	32 A6
William Jameson Pl	28 B3
William St	24 D5
Willow Bank Row	15 G2
Willowbrae Av	27 E4
Willowbrae Gdns	27 F4
Willowbrae Rd	27 E3
Wilsons Park	28 C3
Wilton Rd	40 B5
Windmill La	5 E6
Windmill Pl	5 E6
Windsor Pl	28 C4
Windsor St	26 A2
Windsor St Lane	26 A2
Winton Dri	49 F6
Winton Gro	49 E6
Winton Ter	49 E6
Wishaw Ter	26 D2
Wisp Grn	42 C3
Wolrige Rd	50 C2
Wolseley Cres	27 E3
Wolseley Ter	27 E3
Woodbine Ter	16 C6
Woodburn Ter	39 E4
Woodfield Av	46 D4
Woodfield Park	46 D5
Woodhall Av	46 B5
Woodhall Bank	46 D5
Woodhall Dri	46 A4
Woodhall Gro	46 C5
Woodhall Mill Brae	46 B4
Woodhall Rd	46 C5

Name	Ref
Woodhall Ter	46 A4
Woodlands Grn	27 G6
Woodside Ter	29 E5
Woodstock Pl	50 D1
Woodville Ter	16 C6
Woolmet Cres	52 C2
Worlds End Clo	5 F3
Wrights Houses	39 E1
Wyvern Park	39 G3
Yardheads	16 B4
Yeaman La	38 C1
Yeaman Pl	38 C1
Yewlands Cres	50 D3
Yewlands Gdns	50 D3
York La	25 G2
York Pl	4 D1
York Rd	15 E2
Young St	4 A2
Young St Lane Nth	4 A2
Young St Lane Sth	4 A2
Zetland Pl	14 D3

BILSTON

Name	Ref
Allermuir Av	Inset 60
Brookfield Ter	Inset 60
Burnbank Ter	Inset 60
Caerketton Av	Inset 60
Castlelaw Cres	Inset 60
Eskgrove Dri	Inset 60
Meadow Pl	Inset 60
Moorfoot View	Inset 60
Myrtle Cres	Inset 60
Park Av	Inset 60
Seafield Moor Rd	Inset 60
Seafield Rd	Inset 60
Stanley Av	Inset 60
Woodfield Park	Inset 60

BONNYRIGG

Name	Ref
Almond Cres	57 D3
Argyll Pl	57 B3
Auld Orchard	57 E2
Beech Loan	57 D4
Bellfield View	57 F2
Big Brae	57 D1
Broomieknowe	57 D2
Broomieknowe Gdns	57 D1
Broomieknowe Park	57 D1
Cameron Cres	57 B4
Campview Rd	57 D3
Cherry Rd	57 D3
Chester Gro	57 D4
Chester View	57 D4
Chestnut Gro	57 D4
Church Rd	57 B1
Cockpen Av	57 C4
Cockpen Cres	57 C4
Cockpen Dri	57 C4
Cockpen Pl	57 C4
Cockpen Rd	57 E3
Cockpen Ter	57 C4
Cockpen Vw	57 C4
Cuguen Pl	57 D1
Dalhousie Av	57 C3
Dalhousie Av West	57 C3
Dalhousie Dri	57 C3
Dalhousie Gdns	57 C3
Dalhousie Pl	57 C3
Dalhousie Rd East	57 C3
Dalhousie Rd West	57 C4
De Quincey Path	57 B3
De Quincey Rd	57 A4
Dickson Gro	57 E3
Dobbies Rd	57 C2
Douglas Cres	57 D2
Dundas Pk	57 E3
Dundas St	57 E3
Durham Bank	57 E3
Durham Gro	57 E3
Durham Pl	57 E3
Eldindean Pl	57 D1
Eldindean Rd	57 E2
Eldindean Ter	57 E2
Elm Row	57 D1
Eskbank Rd	57 E2
Eskdale Ct	57 C3
Eskdale DrAi	57 C3
Eskdale Ter	57 C2
Evans Gdns	57 F2
Farm Av	57 B3
Glebe Pl	57 B1

Golf Course Rd
Gordon Av
Hawthornden Av
Hawthornden Gdns
Hazel Dri
High St, Bonnyrigg
High St, Lasswade
Hillhead
Holly Ter
Hopefield Pk
Hopefield Pl
Hopefield Ter
Hunter Ter
James Leary Way
Kevock Rd
Laird Ter
Lasswade Rd
Leyden Pk
Leyden St
Lime Pl
Lothian St
McLean Pl
McQuade St
Martin Gro
Maryfield Pl
Mason Pl
Mavisbank Pl
Mayshade Rd
Melville Dykes Rd
Melville Vw
Methven Ter
Moffat Av
Moore Pl
Moorfoot Vw
Myredale
Park Cres
Park Rd
Parsons Pool
Pendreich Av
Pendreich Dri
Pendreich Gro
Pendreich Ter
Pendreich Vw
Pentland Rd
Polton Av Rd
Polton Bank
Polton Bank Ter
Polton Cotts
Polton Ct
Polton Gdns
Polton Rd
Polton St
Poplar Ter
Pryde Av
Pryde Ter
Quarryfoot Gdns
Quarryfoot Grn
Quarryfoot Dri
Raes Gdns
Ramsay Ter
Rockville Ter
Rosewell Rd
Rowan Gdns
St Anns Av
St Anns Path
School Brae
School Grn
Scollon Av
Seaforth Ter
Sherwood Av
Sherwood Ct
Sherwood Cres
Sherwood Dri
Sherwood Gro
Sherwood Ind Est
Sherwood Loan
Sherwood Pk
Sherwood Ter
Sherwood Vw
Sherwood Walk
Skeltie Muir Av
Skeltie Muir Ct
Skeltie Muir Gro
Union Pk
Upper Broomieknowe
Viewbank Av
Viewbank Cotts
Viewbank Rd
Viewbank Vw
Viewfield
Viewpark Gdns
Wadingburn La
Wadingburn Rd
Walker Pl
Waugh Path
Waverley Cres
Waverley Dri
Waverley Pk

Rd	57 E2	Komarom Pl	56 F2	Barleyknowe Rd	65 B1	Inveravon Rd	53 C4
Ter	57 E3	Langlaw Rd	56 F4	Barleyknowe St	65 B1	Kennington Av	53 B5
	57 D1	Lansbury Ct	56 D1	Barleyknowe Ter	65 B1	Kennington Ter	53 B5
Wynd	57 C1	Larkfield Dri	56 A3	Bonnybank Ct	65 C2	Lasswade Rd	53 D5
on Rd	57 C3	Larkfield Rd	56 A2	Bonnybank Rd	65 C2	Linden Pl	53 D5
Ct	57 C1	Lasswade Rd	56 A2	Braeside Rd Nth	65 C2	*Lomond Walk, Straiton	
ld	57 C1	*Lauder Lodge,		Braeside Rd Sth	65 C3	Caravan Park	53 A4
	57 D3	Newmills Rd	56 D2	Burnside Rd	65 C1	*Lorne Gro, Straiton	
v	57 F2	Lauder Rd	56 E2	Carlowrie Pl	65 C2	Caravan Park	53 A4
	57 F3	Laurel Bank	56 F2	Clearburn Rd	65 B1	McKinlay Ter	53 B5
	57 E3	Little Acre	56 F4	Dalkeith Rd	65 A1	McNeill Av	53 B5
		London Rd	56 C2	Emily Ct	65 B1	McNeill Pl	53 B5

ALKEITH

		Lothian Bank	56 B3	Emily Pl	65 C2	McNeill Ter	53 B5
	56 C3	Lothian Dri	56 E4	Engine Rd	65 E4	Mavisbank	53 C6
ank	56 D1	Lothian Rd	56 C2	Glen View Ct	65 B2	Mayburn Av	53 B5
d	56 B3	Lugton Brae	56 B1	Glen View Cres	65 B2	Mayburn Bank	53 C4
d	56 B3	Martin Pl	56 A2	Glen View Rd	65 B2	Mayburn Ct	53 B4
	56 B2	Maryburn Rd	56 E4	Gore Av	65 C2	Mayburn Cres	53 B4
Av	56 A3	Maxton Ct	56 D1	Greenhall Cres	65 B1	Mayburn Dri	53 B4
	56 A3	Mayfield Rd	56 B1	Greenhall Rd	65 B1	Mayburn Gro	53 B4
Ct	56 E1	Melville Gate Rd	56 A1	Harvieston Villas	65 C3	Mayburn Hill	53 B5
Rd	56 A4	Melville Rd	56 A2	Hillside Cres Nth	65 C2	Mayburn House	53 C4
	56 C1	Melville Ter	56 B3	Hillside Cres Sth	65 C3	Mayburn Loan	53 B4
Ct,		Mitchell St	56 C1	Hogarth Av	65 B1	Mayburn Ter	53 B4
gh Rd	56 C1	Muirpark	56 A4	Hunter Sq	65 C3	Mayburn Vale	53 B5
Dri	56 A3	Musselburgh Rd	56 D1	Hunterfield Ct	65 C2	Mayburn Walk	53 B5
Pk	56 A3	New Mills Ter	56 D1	*Hunterfield Park,		Mayfield Ct	53 D5
s	56 D2	Newbattle Abbey Cres	56 B4	Hunterfield Rd	65 A1	Mayfield Cres	53 C5
Clo	56 C1	Newbattle Rd	56 B3	Hunterfield Rd	65 A1	Mayshade Rd	53 B4
St	56 C1	Newmills Rd	56 C2	Hunterfield Ter	65 A1	Muirfield Gdns	53 C5
es	56 E4	Newton St	56 E4	Jubilee Cres	65 B1	New Pentland Ind Est	53 A6
Rd	56 B2	North Wynd	56 C1	Juner Pl	65 C1	Nivens Knowe Rd	53 A6
dns	56 F2	Old Dalkeith Rd	56 A1	Kirkhill Ter	65 A1	Paradykes Av	53 B5
Dri	56 A3	Old Edinburgh Rd	56 C1	Lady Brae	65 C3	Park Av	53 B6
Gro	56 A3	Orchard Vw	56 A2	Lady Brae Pl	65 D3	Park Cres	53 B6
Pk	56 A3	Pankhurst Loan	56 F2	Laundry Cotts	65 B1	Park View	53 B6
Ter	56 A3	Park Cres	56 F2	McLean Pl	65 C2	Pentland Rd	53 A5
Rd	56 F1	Park Rd	56 B3	Main St	65 C3	Polton Rd	53 C6
res	56 F1	Parkhead Park	56 E4	Mossend Cotts	65 D3	Station Rd	53 C5
ro	56 F1	Parkhead Pl	56 E4	New Hunterfield	65 B1	Straiton Retail	
a	56 F2	Parkside Pl	56 C2	Newbyres Av	65 B1	Centre	53 B4
ark	56 F2	Pentland Vw,		Newbyres Cres	65 C2	Straiton Rd	53 A5
er	56 F1	Easthouses	56 F1	Oaklea Cotts	65 D2	The Loan	53 B6
w	56 F1	Pentland Vw,		Parkhill	65 B2	Traprain Ter	53 D6
	56 A2	Thornybank	56 F2	Povert Rd	65 A1		
	56 C2	Pettigrews Clo	56 C1	Private Rd	65 C3		

LONGNIDDRY

unt	56 C1	Place Charente	56 E2	Quarry Rd	65 C1		
Rd	56 B4	Primrose Cres	56 E2	Redheugh Loan	65 B1	Amisfield Pl	65 C5
	56 C1	Primrose Ter	56 E2	Springfield Pl	65 C3	Campbell Ct	65 B5
es	56 A3	Roanshead Rd	56 E4	Station Rd	65 C3	Campbell Rd	65 B5
ro	56 A3	Robert Burns Meadows	56 F2	Swan Cres	65 C2	Charteris Ct	65 C5
l	56 A3	St Andrew St	56 C1	The Avenue	65 B1	Charteris Pk	65 C5
s Pl	56 F4	Salters Gro	56 E1	Victoria St	65 A1	Charteris Rd	65 B5
s Rd	56 F3	Salters Rd	56 E1	Vogrie Cres	65 C3	Church Gdns	65 C5
s Way	56 F4	Salters Ter	56 E1	Vogrie Cres Sth	65 C3	Church Way	65 C5
Rd	56 C1	Shadepark Cres	56 D1	Vogrie Pl	65 C3	Cotlands Av	65 B6
ank	56 D2	Shadepark Dri	56 D1	Vogrie Rd	65 C3	Cotlands Pk	65 B6
	56 D2	Shadepark Gdns	56 D1	Wilson Rd	65 C1	Cunningham Ct	65 B6
ark	56 D2	South St	56 C1			Dean Ct	65 B6
d	56 D1	Spalding Cres	56 E2			Dean Park	65 B6
	56 C1	Station Rd	56 B3			Dean Rd	65 A5

LOANHEAD

y-Pass	56 A4	Strawberry Bank	56 B3			Douglas Cres	65 C4
d	56 B2	Tait St	56 C1	Academy La	53 D5	Douglas Rd	65 C4
er	56 B3	Taylor Rd	56 F2	Arbuthnot Rd	53 D5	East Campbell Ct	65 C5
	56 C1	Walker Cres	56 A3	Bilston Glen	53 A6	Elcho Ct	65 C5
ro	56 B1	Waterfall Walk	56 E2	Braeside Rd	53 D5	Elcho Rd	65 C5
llas	56 B2	Waverley Rd	56 B2	Buller Cres	53 D5	Elcho Ter	65 C5
Villas	56 A3	Weir Cres	56 A2	Burghlee Cres	53 C6	Forthview Rd	65 C4
t	56 D1	Westfield Ct	56 A3	Burghlee Ter	53 C6	Glassel Park Rd	65 B6
idns	56 D1	Westfield Dri	56 A3	*Burndene Dri, Straiton		Gosford Rd	65 C5
d	56 C2	Westfield Gro	56 A3	Caravan Park	53 A4	John Knox Rd	65 C5
er	56 D1	Westfield Pk	56 A3	Church St	53 C5	Kings Av	65 B6
	56 E1	Wheatsheaf La	56 D1	Clerk St	53 C5	Kings Ct	65 B5
Rd	56 A1	Whitehill Dri	56 F2	Dalum Ct	53 B5	Kings Gro	65 B5
	56 C1	Whitehill Gro	56 F2	Dalum Dri	53 B5	Kings Park	65 B5
es	56 B2	Wilson Av	56 E1	Dalum Gro	53 B5	Kings Rd	65 B5
Cres	56 F4	Wishart Pl	56 E2	Dalum Loan	53 B5	Kitchener Cres	65 C5
ri	56 E2	Woodburn Av	56 E2	Dryden Av	53 A6	Links Rd	65 C5
	56 E2	Woodburn Bank	56 E1	Dryden Cres	53 A6	Lyars Rd	65 C4
	56 C1	Woodburn Dri	56 D2	Dryden Ter	53 B5	Main Rd	65 B6

AL ESTATES:

		Woodburn Gdns	56 E2	Dryden View	53 A6	Main St	65 C5
ses Ind Est	56 F4	Woodburn Gro	56 E2	Edgefield Pl	53 C4	Neidpath Ct	65 C5
s Park		Woodburn Loan	56 E2	Edgefield Rd	53 C4	Old Dean Ct	65 B6
t	56 C1	Woodburn Medway	56 F2	Engine Rd	53 C5	Old School La	65 C5
reen Ind Est	56 A4	Woodburn Park	56 E2	Foundry La	53 D4	Orchard Ct	65 B6
ank Ind Est	56 F1	Woodburn Pl	56 F2	Fountain Pl	53 C4	Parkview	65 D5
d	56 B1	Woodburn Rd	56 E1	Fowler Sq	53 D5	School Grn	65 C5
n Av	56 D2	Woodburn St	56 E2	Gaynor Av	53 B5	Seton Rd	65 C5
ur Dri	56 F2	Woodburn Ter	56 F2	George Av	53 C5	Stevenson Ct	65 B6
	56 A2	Woodburn Vw	56 F2	George Cres	53 C5	Stevenson Pk	65 B6
Dri	56 E3			George Dri	53 C5	Stevenson Way	65 B6
Gdns	56 E3			George Ter	53 B5	The Canty	65 B6

GOREBRIDGE

Medway	56 E3			Goldie Ter	53 B6	Wemyss Pl	65 D4
Park	56 F4	Arnprior Rd	65 C3	Hawthorn Gdns	53 B4	Wemyss Rd	65 C4
Rd	56 E3	Barleyknowe Cres	65 B1	Herd Ter	53 A6		
Walk	56 E3	Barleyknowe Gdns	65 B1	High St	53 C5		
		Barleyknowe La	65 B2	Hunter Av	53 D5		
		Barleyknowe Pl	65 B1	Hunter Ct	53 D5		
				Hunter Ter	53 D5		

MUSSELBURGH/WALLYFORD

Albert Cres	31 H3	Fairways	30 C5
Albert Pl	31 H3	Fa'side Av Nth	31 G4
Ashgrove Pl	31 E2	Fa'side Av	31 G4
Ashgrove	31 E2	Fa'side Ct	31 H4
Ashgrove Vw	31 E2	Fa'side Cres	31 G4
Balcarres Pl	30 D1	Fa'side Dri	31 G4
Balcarres Rd	30 D1	Fa'side Gdns	31 H4
Beach La	30 B1	Fa'side Ter	31 H4
Beaulah	31 E2	Ferguson Ct	30 C5
Beggers Bush	31 G1	Ferguson Dri	30 C5
Bellfield Av	30 B2	Ferguson Gdns	30 C5
Bellfield Ct	30 B3	Ferguson Grn	30 C5
Bog Park Rd	30 A2	Ferguson View	30 C5
Bridge St	30 C2	Fishers Wynd	30 B2
Bush St	30 B1	Forthview Av	31 G3
Bush Ter	30 B2	Forthview Cres	31 G3
Cairds Vw	30 B1	Forthview Dri	31 G3
Campie Gdns	30 B2	Forthview Ter	31 G3
Campie Rd	30 B2	Galt Cres	31 F3
Carberry Rd	30 D4	Galt Dri	31 G2
Carly Pl	30 C2	Galt Rd	31 G3
Champigny Ct	31 E3	Galt Ter	31 G3
Church La	30 C3	Goose Grn	30 D1
Clayknowes Av	30 A3	Goose Grn Av	30 D1
Clayknowes Ct	30 A4	Goose Grn Cres	30 D1
Clayknowes Cres	30 A3	Goose Grn Pl	30 D1
Clayknowes Dri	30 A3	Goose Grn Rd	30 D1
Clayknowes Way	30 A3	Gracefield Ct	30 C2
Cottage La	31 E3	Greenfield Park	30 B5
Cowpits Rd	30 D6	Grove St	30 D3
Cowpits Ford Rd	30 C5	Haddington Rd	31 G2
Craighill Ter	31 F2	Harbour Rd	30 B2
Crookston Rd	31 E4	Hercus Loan	30 B2
Dalrymple Cres	30 A2	High St	30 C2
Dalrymple Loan	30 C2	Hope Pl	31 F2
Delta Av	31 F3	Inchview Cres	31 H3
Delta Cres	31 G2		
Delta Dri	31 G2		
Delta Gdns	31 G3		
Delta Pl	30 D4		
Delta Rd	31 G3		
Delta Vw	31 G2		
Denholm Rd	30 A3		
Denholm Way	30 A3		
Double Dykes	30 D4		
Downie Pl	30 C2		
Drummohr Av	31 G3		
Drummohr Gdns	31 G3		
Edenhall Bank	31 E3		
Edenhall Cres	31 E3		
Edenhall Rd	31 E3		
Edinburgh Rd	30 A1		
Eskmill Villas	30 B3		
Eskside East	30 C2		
Eskside West	30 B3		
Eskview Av	30 B3		
Eskview Cres	30 B3		
Eskview Gro	30 B3		
Eskview Rd	30 B3		
Eskview Ter	30 B3		

Inchview Rd 31 H3
INDUSTRIAL ESTATES:
Fisherrow Ind Est 30 A2
Inveravon Ter 30 C3
Inveresk Rd 30 C3
Inveresk Village Rd 30 D3
James St 30 D2
Kerrswynd 30 D2
Kilwinning Pl 30 D2
Kilwinning St 30 D2
Kilwinning Ter 30 D2
King St 30 D3
Ladywell 30 C2
Ladywell Way 30 C2
Lewisvale Av 31 E3
Lewisvale Ct 31 E3
Linkfield Ct 31 E2
Linkfield Rd 30 D2
Links Av 30 B1
Links St 30 C2
Links View 30 C1
Lochend Rd Nth 30 B2
Lochend Rd Sth 30 B2
Lorretto Ct 30 B4
Macbeth Moir Rd 31 F2
Maitland Av 30 A2
Maitland Park 30 A2
Maitland Rd 30 A2
Maitland St 30 A2
Mall Av 30 C2
Mansfield Av 30 D3
Mansfield Ct 30 D3
Mansfield Pl 30 C3
Mansfield Rd 30 C2
Market St 30 B2
Mayfield Av 30 B5
Mayfield Cres 30 B4
Mayfield Park 30 B5
Mayfield Pl 30 B5
Mayville Bank 31 G2
Millhill 30 D2
Millhill La 30 D2
Miners Ter 31 H3
Moir Av 31 G2
Moir Cres 31 G2
Moir Dri 31 G2
Moir Pl 31 G2
Moir Ter 31 F2
Monktonhall Pl 30 B5
Monktonhall Ter 30 B4
Mountjoy Ter 30 C1
Mucklets Av 30 A4
Mucklets Ct 30 A4
Mucklets Cres 30 B4
Mucklets Dri 30 A4
Mucklets Pl 30 A4
Musselburgh By-Pass 30 A5
New St 30 D2
Newbigging 30 D2
Newhailes Av 30 A2
Newhailes Cres 30 A2
Newhailes Rd 30 A2
North High St 30 B2
Old Craighall Rd 30 B5
Olive Bank Rd 30 A2
Park Av 31 E3
Park Ct 31 E3
Park Grove Pl 31 E3
Park Grove Ter 31 E3
Park La 31 E3
Park Vw 31 E3
Pinkie Av 31 E3
Pinkie Hill Cres 31 E3
Pinkie Pl 31 E3
Pinkie Rd 30 D3
Pinkie Ter 31 E3
Promenade 30 B1
Ravenshaugh Cres 31 G2
Ravenshaugh Rd 31 F2
Riverside Gdns 30 B3
Rothesay Pl 30 B3
St Clements Gdns Nth 31 H4
St Clements Gdns Sth 31 H4
St Clements Ter 31 H4
St Michaels Av 30 C3
Salters Rd 31 F6
Short Hope St 30 C2
Smeaton Gro 30 D4
South St 30 C2
Station Rd 30 B3
Stoneybank Av 30 B4
Stoneybank Ct 30 B3
Stoneybank Cres 30 A3
Stoneybank Cres 30 B4
Stoneybank Dri 30 B3
Stoneybank Gdns 30 A3
Stoneybank Gdns Nth 30 B3
Stoneybank Gdns Sth 30 B3
Stoneybank Gro 30 B4
Stoneybank Pl 30 B4

Stoneybank Rd 30 B4
Stoneybank Ter 30 B4
Stoneyhill Av 30 A3
Stoneyhill Ct 30 A3
Stoneyhill Dri 30 A3
Stoneyhill Farm Rd 30 B3
Stoneyhill Gro 30 A3
Stoneyhill Pl 30 A3
Stoneyhill Rise 30 A3
Stoneyhill Road 30 A3
Stoneyhill Ter 30 A3
The Grove 31 E3
The Parsonage 30 D2
Watts Clo 30 B2
Wedderburn Ter 30 D4
Wemyss Gdns 31 H3
West Holmes Gdns 30 B2
Whitehill Av 30 A3
Whitehill Gdns 30 A4
Whitehill Rd 30 A4
Windsor Gdns 31 E2
Windsor Park 31 F2
Windsor Park Dri 31 F2
Windsor Park Ter 31 E2
Windy Wynd 30 D4
Woodside Gdns 31 E2

NEWTONGRANGE MAYFIELD

Anderson Av 58 C2
Andrew Dodds Av 58 E1
Ash Gro 58 E1
Beechgrove Rd 58 E2
Beechwood Park 58 B2
Bevan Rd 58 E3
Beveridge Av 58 F3
Beveridge Clo 58 F3
Blackcot Av 58 D3
Blackcot Dri 58 D3
Blackcot Pl 58 D3
Blackcot Rd 58 D3
Bogwood Ct 58 E1
Bogwood Rd 58 D1
Broadhurst Rd 58 D1
Bryans Av 58 B2
Bryans Rd 58 B2
Buckie Rd 58 E2
Burnside Av 58 D1
Burnside Cres 58 D1
Camp Rd 58 F2
Camp Wood Vw 58 E3
Cherry La 58 F2
Chester Vw 58 D3
Conifer Rd 58 E1
Cook Cres 58 E3
Coronation Pl 58 D1
Corrie Ct 58 B4
Crawless Cres 58 E2
Dalhousie Rd 58 A2
*Dalton Ct,
  McKinnon Dri 58 F3
Darcy Rd 58 E2
David Scott Av 58 E1
Dean Park 58 A3
Dean Park Pl 58 A3
Dougal Pl 58 E3
Easthouses Rd 58 D2
Eighth St 58 B3
Elm Pl 58 E2
Eskview Rd 58 D2
Ferguson Way 58 B4
Fifth St 58 B3
Finlay Pl 58 F2
First St 58 B4
Fourth St 58 B3
Galadale Abbey Gra 58 B2
Galadale Cres 58 B2
Galadale Dri 58 B2
Gardiner Pl 58 B2
Gordon St 58 D1
Hamilton Cres 58 C2
Hawthorn Cres 58 D1
Higginson Loan 58 F3
Hill Pl 58 E3
Holly Bank 58 E1
Hughes Cres 58 F2
Hursted Av 58 D1
INDUSTRIAL ESTATES:
  Butlerfield Ind Est 58 A4
  Newbattle Ind Est 58 C3
John Humble St 58 E3
Kier Hardie Dri 58 E3
Kippielaw Park 58 D1
Laburnum Pl 58 E2
Langlaw Rd 58 E1
Larch Cres 58 F2
Laurel Bank Pl 58 E2

Laurel Bank Rd 58 E2
Lawfield Rd 58 E1
Leighton Cres 58 D1
Lilac Av 58 F2
Lime Gro 58 F2
Lingerwood Cotts 58 B4
Lingerwood Farm Cotts 58 C4
Lingerwood Rd 58 B4
Lingerwood Walk 58 B4
Lothian Ter 58 B4
McCathie Dri 58 C2
McDiarmid Gro 58 B4
McGahey Ct 58 B4
McKinnon Dri 58 F3
McLean Walk 58 C4
McTaggart Way 58 C4
Maesterton Pl 58 B4
Main St 58 A3
Mansfield Av 58 B2
Mansfield Pl 58 B2
Mansfield Rd 58 B2
Mayfield Pl 58 E2
Mayfield Rd 58 D1
Monks Wood 58 B3
Monkswood Rd 58 B4
Morris Rd 58 C2
Murderdean Rd 58 A2
Myrtle Gro 58 E1
New Star Bank 58 A3
Newbattle Rd 58 A1
Ninth St 58 B3
Oak Cres 58 E2
Oak Pl 58 F2
Old Star Bank 58 A3
Park Rd 58 B2
Pinewood Pl 58 E2
Pinewood Rd 58 E2
Pinewood View 58 E2
Poplar St 58 F2
Ramsay Cres 58 E3
Ramsay Walk 58 F3
Redwood Gro 58 A3
Redwood Walk 58 A3
Reed Dri 58 C2
Robert Smille Av 58 E3
Ross Pl 58 B2
Rowantree Rd 58 E2
Ruskin Pl 58 E3
St Annes Ct 58 B3
St Davids 58 B3
Salisbury View 58 E2
Saugh Cotts 58 B4
Second St 58 B4
Seventh St 58 B3
Sixth St 58 B3
Smithy Cotts 58 C4
Station Rd 58 A3
Steele Av 58 F2
Stevenson La 58 B4
Stobhill Rd 58 B4
Stone Av 58 E2
Stone Pl 58 D3
Suttieslea Cres 58 D2
Suttieslea Dri 58 C2
Suttieslea Pl 58 C2
Suttieslea Rd 58 C2
Suttieslea Walk 58 C2
Sycamore Rd 58 E2
Tenth St 58 B2
The Beeches 58 B1
The Square 58 B3
Third St 58 B3
Victoria Gdns 58 A3
Victoria Rd 58 A3
Watt Gro 58 F3
Waverley Pk 58 D2
Waverley St 58 D3
Waverley Ter 58 D2
Westhouses Av 58 F3
Westhouses Dri 58 E3
Westhouses Rd 58 E3
Westhouses St 58 E3
Willow Rd 58 F2

PENICUIK

Alderbank 61 D8
Andrew Clo 61 C5
Ann St 61 C5
Armine Pl 61 F5
Arrass Gro 60 E4
Assynt Bank 61 E6
Avon Gro 61 E6
Baldwin Ct 61 C8
Balfour Ter 60 F3
Bank St 61 D7
Bavelaw Cres 61 B6
Beech Pl 61 D8

Bellmans Rd 61 C6
Belwood Cres 60 F3
Belwood Rd 60 C3
Blenheim Ct 60 E4
Bog Rd 61 C7
Boyd-Orr Dri 60 K4
Braidlaw Park 61 A7
Breck Ter 60 E4
Bridge St 61 D8
Brockwood Av 61 A6
Broomhill Av 61 C7
Broomhill Rd 61 C8
Brunstane Gdns 61 B6
Cairnbank Gdns 61 C8
Cairnbank Rd 61 C8
Caplan Way 61 A7
Carlops Av 61 C6
Carlops Cres 61 C6
Carlops Rd 61 A7
Carnethy Av 61 D6
Carnethy Ct 61 D6
Castlelaw Ct 61 D6
Catriona Ter 60 F3
Charles St 61 C5
Chisholm Ter 61 D5
Clerk Rd 61 B7
Corunna Ter 60 E4
Cowan Ter 61 D5
Craigfield Cres 61 C8
Cranston St 61 C7
Crockett Gdns 61 B7
Croft St 61 C8
Cruachan Ct 61 E6
Cuiken Av 61 C6
Cuiken Bank 61 B6
Cuiken Ter 61 B6
Cuikenburn 61 C5
Dean Pl 61 B6
Dean Rd 61 B6
Deanburn 61 B5
Dick Ter 61 D6
Dykes Rd 61 C5
East Queensway 61 D5
Eastfield 61 D6
Eastfield Dri 61 D6
Eastfield Farm Rd 61 D5
Eastfield Park Rd 61 D6
Edinburgh Rd 61 D6
Esk Bridge 61 E6
Eskhill 61 D6
Eskmill Rd 61 E7
Eskvale Cres 61 E6
Eskvale Dri 61 E6
Ewing St 61 D5
Fetteresk Cotts 61 C8
Fletcher Gro 60 D4
Friarton Gdns 61 A7
Gardners Walk 61 A6
Glaskill Ter 61 C6
Glen Pl 61 C6
Glencross Gdns 61 A7
Glenview 61 C6
Grahams Rd 60 F3
Greenhill Park 61 C6
Greenlaw Gro 60 E3
Grieve Ct 61 D5
Harkerburn Gdns 61 A6
Harpers Brae 61 D6
Hawkins Ter 60 F4
*Heinsberg House,
  John St 61 C6
High St 61 D7
Hill View 61 E6
Imrie Pl 61 D7
INDUSTRIAL ESTATES:
  Eastfield Ind Est 61 D6
  Eskmill Ind Est 61 E7
Inkerman St 60 E4
Jackson St 61 C7
John Knox Pl 61 D7
John St 61 C6
Johnson 60 D4
Kirk View 61 D7
Kirkhill Gdns 61 D7
Kirkhill Rd 61 D7
Kirklands 61 C7
Kirkton Bank 61 B7
Knightslaw Pl 61 B7
Laing Ter 61 D5
Laverock Dri 61 B5
Lawers Sq 61 E5
Lawhead Pl 61 A6
Lawrie Dri 61 C5
Ledi Ter 61 E5
Livesay Ter 60 E4
Loanburn 61 C7
Loanburn Av 61 D6
Lomond Vale 61 E5

Lowrie Av
Lyne Ter
MacCormick Ter
Marchburn Dri
Mauricewood Av
Mauricewood Bank
Mauricewood Gro
Mauricewood Park
Mauricewood Rise
Mauricewood Road
Meggat Pl
Merlyon Way
Monksrig Rd
Moorfoot Pl
Muirhead Pl
Namur Rd
Nevis Gdns
Peebles Rd
Pentland Av
Pentland Ter
Philip Pl
Pomathorn Bank
Pomathorn Rd
Queensway
Ramillies Ct
Ramsay Pl
Ravelsykes Rd
Ravendean Gdns
Red Fox Cres
Royal Ct
Rullion Grn Av
Rullion Grn Cnr
Rullion Rd
St James Gdns
St James Vw
St Kentigern Rd
St Kentigern Way
St Mungos View
Salamanca Cres
Samoa Ter
Scott Rd
Shaws Ct
Silverburn Dri
Stevenson Rd
Strathesk Gro
Strathesk Pl
Strathesk Rd
Tait Dri
Terregles
Teviot Gro
The Quadrant
The Square
Thornburn
Trelawney Ter
Valleyfield Rd
Valleyfield View
Vaucluse Pl
Vorlich Cres
Watson St
Waulkmill Dri
Waulkmill Rd
Waulkmill View
West Cairn Cres
West St
Wilson St
Windsor Cres
Windsor Dri
Windsor Rd
Windsor Sq
Windsor Ter
Woodside Dri
Wyvis Park
Yarrow Ct

PRESTONPANS PORT SETON COCKENZIE

Acheson Dri
Alexander Dri
Ash Park
*Aldhammer Ho,
  Seaside
Avenue Rd
Ayres Wynd
Bankton Ter
Barracks St
Bayview
Beech Cres
Bellfield Sq
Burnside
Cadell Pl
Castle Av
Castle Rd
Castle Ter
Castle Vw
Castle Walk
Cedar Dri

/ Rd	62 C4
	62 C4
	63 E2
d	62 A5
q	62 A5
ts	62 C5
	62 A5
	62 C6
	63 E2
g	62 A5
e Dri	62 A6
	62 C4
ner Pl	63 E2
n Rd	62 C3
	63 E2
d	63 F2
s	63 G2
is	63 G2
	63 G2
nd	63 G2
t	62 C4
s Clo	63 E2
Cres	62 D5
Rd	62 C5
Ter	62 C6
lk	62 A5
ns	62 C5
	63 F2
d	63 E2
Walk	63 E2
res East	62 B5
res West	62 B5
ro	62 B5
d	62 B5
ool Cnr	62 B5
	63 E2
ll	62 C4
ll Gdns	62 C4
Bank	62 D2
Rd	62 D5
Ter	62 D2
ort Seton	62 D2
restonpans	62 A5
	62 A5
Nth	62 A5
AL ESTATES:	
ad (Prestonpans)	
st	62 B6
ark Ind Est	62 D3
	63 E2
opes Rd	62 C6
Ter	63 F2
	63 E2
St	62 B4
	62 B4
	63 F2
	63 G2
	63 F2
	63 G2
	63 G2
	62 D4
	62 D4
k Rd	62 A5
s	62 B5
	63 E2
	63 F3
St	62 D2
hill Cotts	63 E5
	62 A6
t Sq	62 D4
	62 B4
t Rd	62 C4
ort Seton	63 E2
restonpans	62 A5
	62 C5
k Rd	62 A5
s	62 C5
nge Av	62 B5
nge Gro	62 B5
nge Rd	62 B5
Walk	62 A5
n Park	63 E2
	62 B6
Ct	62 B5
Gdns	62 B5
res	62 B5
Pl	62 B4
r	63 E2
r	62 C5
Walk	62 A5

Park Rd	63 F1
Park View	62 D5
Park View East	63 F2
Park View West	63 F2
Polwarth Cres	62 C4
Polwarth Ter	62 C5
Preston Av	62 D5
Preston Ct	62 B6
Preston Cres	62 D4
Preston Cross Cotts	62 C5
Preston Rd	62 B6
Preston Rd	62 D5
Preston Ter	62 D5
Preston Tower	62 C5
Prestongrange Rd	62 A5
Prestongrange Ter	62 A5
Pypers Wynd	62 C4
Redburn Rd	62 A5
Rigley Ter	62 A6
Ringans Gdns	62 B4
Ringans Way	62 A5
Robertson Av	62 C4
Rope Walk	62 A5
Rose Mount	62 B4
Rowan Gro	62 E3
*Salt Preston Pl,	
Seaside	62 B5
Schaw Rd	62 D4
School La	63 E2
Seaside East	62 B4
Seaside West	62 B4
Seton Ct	63 G2
Seton Pl	63 F2
Seton Vw	63 G2
Seton Wynd	63 G2
Sir Walter Scott Pend	62 C4
South Cres	62 C5
South Doors	63 E2
South Grange Av	62 B6
South Lorimer Pl	63 E3
South Seton Park	63 E2
South View	62 C5
Station Rd	62 C6
Summerlee	62 A5
The Pottery	62 A5
Thompson Cres	63 E2
Thorntree Cres	62 D5
Tranent By-Pass	62 D6
Turret Gdns	62 B6
Viewforth	63 E2
Wemyss Pl	63 E2
West Harbour Rd	62 D2
West Loan	62 B5
West Loan Ct	62 B5
West Long Craigs	63 G2
West Lorimer Pl	62 D2
Whin Park	62 D3
Wilson Av	62 C5
Winton Loan	63 H4
Winton Pk	63 E2
Woodbine Gdns	62 B5

QUEENSFERRY

Almond Gro	6 D4
Arrol Pl	6 D3
Ashburnham Gdns	7 E3
Ashburnham Rd	7 E3
Atheling Gro	6 D4
Bankhead Gro	7 E3
Bo'Ness Rd	6 A3
Builyeon Rd	6 A3
Burgess Rd	6 D3
Canmore St	6 C3
Carlowrie Av	7 E4
Carlowrie Cres	7 E4
Carmelite Rd	6 C3
Cluflatt	6 A2
Cluflatt Brae	6 A2
Dundas Av	6 D3
Echline	6 A3
Echline Av	6 A3
Echline Dri	6 A3
Echline Gdns	6 A3
Echline Grn	6 A3
Echline Gro	6 B2
Echline Park	6 B3
Echline Pl	6 B3

Echline Rigg	6 B2
Echline Ter	6 B3
Echline Vw	6 B3
Edinburgh Rd	6 D2
Farquar Ter	6 B2
Ferryburn Grn	6 D3
Ferrymuir La	6 C4
Forth Pl	6 B2
Forth Rd Bridge	6 C2
Forth Ter	7 E3
Gote La	6 C2
Harbour La	6 C2
Hawes Brae	7 E2
Hawthorn Bank	6 C2
Henry Ross Pl	6 C3
High St	6 D2
Hillwood Pl	6 C2
Hope St	6 C3
Hopetoun Rd	6 C2
Hugh Russell Pl	6 C3
Inchcolm Ter	6 C3
Inchgarvie Park	6 B2
Inchkeith Av	6 D3
John Mason Ct	6 D3
Kempston Pl	6 D4
Kirkliston Rd	6 C3
Lawson Cres	6 D3
Loch Pl	6 C3
Loch Rd	6 C3
Long Crook	6 B3
Lovers La	6 D4
Main St	7 F4
Morison Gdns	6 C2
Moubray Gro	6 D4
Newhalls Rd	7 E2
Ochill Ct	6 D3
Plewlandcroft	6 C2
Plewlands Pl	6 C3
Primrose Gdns	6 D3
Priory Grn	6 C3
Provost Milne Gro	6 D4
Queen Margaret Dri	6 D3
Rose La	6 C2
Rosebery Av	6 D3
Rosebery Ct	6 D3
Rosehil Ter	7 E3
School La	6 D3
Scotstoun Av	6 D4
Scotstoun Grn	6 C4
Scotstoun Park	6 D4
Shore Rd	6 C2
Society Rd	6 B2
Sommerville Gdns	7 E4
South Scotstoun	6 D4
Springfield Cres	6 A3
Springfield Lea	6 A2
Springfield Pl	6 A2
Springfield Rd	6 A2
Springfield Ter	6 A3
Springfield View	6 B2
Springwell Pl	6 C2
Standingstane Rd	7 F4
Station Rd	6 D3
Stewart Clark Av	6 D3
Stewart Ter	6 C2
Stoneycroft Rd	6 D2
Stoneyflatts	6 B3
Stoneyflatts Cres	6 B3
The Glebe	7 E4
The Loan	6 C2
Vennel	6 D2
Viewforth Rd	6 C3
Villa Rd	6 C2
Walker Dri	6 B2
Whitehead Grn	6 D3
William Black Pl	6 D3

ROSLIN & ROSEWELL

Carnethie St	59 E4
Chapel Loan	59 B2
Charlton Gro	59 A2
Cochrina Pl	59 E3
Crusader Dri	59 A2
Dean Ter	59 E4
Dryden Gro	59 B2
Duke St	59 E4
Gorton Loan	59 E3

Gorton Pl	59 E3
Gorton Rd	59 D3
Gorton Walk	59 E3
Greenside Pl	59 E3
Gunpowder La	59 A3
Hospital Rd	59 F2
Knowetop Pl	59 A2
Lockhart Ter	59 A2
Lothian St	59 E3
Luisa Sq	59 E3
Main St	59 A1
Manse Rd	59 B2
Marmion Av	59 A2
Minstrel Ct	59 B2
Moat View	59 A2
Nobel Pl	59 A2
Penicuik Rd	59 A2
Pentland Cres	59 E3
Pentland View Cres	59 A2
Pentland View Pl	59 A2
Pentland View Rd	59 A2
Pentland View Ter	59 A2
Prestonhall Cres	59 E3
Prestonhall Rd	59 E3
Prestonhall St	59 E3
Private Rd	59 A4
Roseabelle Rd	59 A2
Rosewell Rd	59 F2
Rossglen Ct	59 B2
St Clair Cres	59 B2
Springfield Pl	59 B2
Station Rd	59 B2
Thornton Rd	59 E4
Victoria St	59 E3
Wallace Cres	59 B2
Whitehill Rd	59 E4
Woodend Park	59 A2

TRANENT

Annfield	64 E3
Balfour Sq	64 D2
Bankpark Brae	64 B1
Bankpark Cres	64 B1
Bankpark Gro	64 C1
Birsley Rd	64 C2
Blawearie Rd	64 D2
Brickworks Rd	64 B1
Bridge St	64 C2
Cadell Sq	64 D2
Caesar Rd	64 C2
Caesar Way	64 C2
Caponhall Ct	64 C3
Caponhall Dri	64 C3
Caponhall Rd	64 C3
Caponhall Way	64 C2
Carlaverock Av	64 E3
Carlaverock Clo	64 E3
Carlaverock Ct	64 D3
Carlaverock Cres	64 D3
Carlaverock Dri	64 D3
Carlaverock Gro	64 D3
Carlaverock Ter	64 D3
Carlaverock View	64 D3
Carlaverock Walk	64 C3
Castle Rd	64 C3
Church St	64 C1
Civic Sq	64 C2
Coal Neuk	64 C2
Coalgate Av	64 E1
Coalgate Rd	64 D1
Co-operative Bldgs	64 D2
Coronation Pl	64 C2
Dequincey Walk	64 C3
Dovecote Brae	64 C3
Duncan Gdns	64 C1
Edinburgh Rd	64 A2
Elder St	64 C1
Elphinstone Ct	64 B3
Elphinstone Rd	64 B4
Fa'side Av	64 D3
Fa'side Cres	64 D3
Fa'side Rd	64 D3
Fleet Rd	64 C3
Fleets Gro	64 D4
Fleets View	64 D4
Forsters Vw	64 D2

Fowler St	64 C1
Gardners Pl	64 C1
George Walk	64 C2
George Way	64 C2
Glennie Gdns	64 D2
Haddington Rd	64 E2
Harkness Cres	64 D2
Henderson Gdns	64 D2
High St	64 C2
Hope Pl	64 D1
Hungerage Sq	64 D3
John Kerr Cres	64 C2
Johnnie Copes Rd	64 A1
Kerr Way	64 C2
Kings Rd	64 C3
Kingslaw Ct	64 D2
Lammermoor Gdns	64 B2
Lammermoor Ter	64 B2
Lammerview	64 D3
Lindores Dri	64 D2
Loch Rd	64 D2
Loch Sq	64 D2
McNeill Path	64 C2
McNeill Walk	64 C2
McNeill Way	64 C3
McPhail Sq	64 C2
Meeting House Dri	64 C2
Millar	64 C3
Morrison Av	64 E2
Muirpark Ct	64 E3
Muirpark Dri	64 E3
Muirpark Gdns	64 E3
Muirpark Gro	64 E3
Muirpark Pl	64 E3
Muirpark Rd	64 E3
Muirpark Ter	64 E3
Muirpark Wynd	64 E3
Muirside Dri	64 C3
New Rd	64 C2
New St	64 C1
Northfield	64 E2
Northfield East	64 E2
Ormiston Cres East	64 E2
Ormiston Cres West	64 E2
Ormiston Rd	64 D2
Ormiston View	64 E2
Pinkie Walk	64 B3
Polson Gdns	64 B2
Post Rd	64 B1
Robertson Av	64 D2
Robertson Dri	64 D1
Ross Cres	64 D2
St Martins La	64 D2
Sandersons Gro	64 D1
Sandersons Wynd	64 D1
Seton Ct	64 B3
Stair Park	64 B1
Steil Gro	64 C3
Swan Rd	64 C3
The Butts	64 C2
The Heugh	64 C1
The Orchard	64 C1
Tranent By-Pass	64 A1
Viewforth Gdns	64 C2
Viewforth Ter	64 C2
Wallace Pl	64 C1
Well Wynd	64 D2
West Windygoul	64 C3
West Windygoul Gdns	64 C3
Wilson Walk	64 C3
Windygoul Cres	64 E3
Winton Clo	64 E4
Winton Ct	64 E4
Winton Gro	64 E4
Winton Pl	64 D2
Winton Way	64 D3
Young Av	64 D3

LIST OF PLACES OF INTEREST TO EDINBURGH CENTRE MAP (pages 4 & 5)

Acheson House,
Craft Centre   5 G3
Adam House Theatre (1) 5 E4
Albert Memorial   4 A3
Appleton Tower   5 E6
Argyle House   4 B5
Assembly Rooms
  & Music Hall   4 B2
Burns Monument   5 G2
Bus Station   4 D1
Calton Cemetery   5 E2
Calton Hill   5 F1
Calton New
  Burial Ground   5 G2
Canongate Kirk (2)   5 G3
Canongate Tollbooth,
  Brass Rubbing Centre 5 G3
Castle Bank   4 B4
Cat Nick   5 H5
Central Library   4 D4
Chalmers Hospital   4 B6
Childhood Museum (3) 5 E3
City Art Centre   4 D3
City Chambers   4 D3
College of Art   4 B5
Conservation Centre   4 C1
Crown Office   5 G2
David Hume Tower   5 E6
Deaconess Hospital   5 F5
Dental School   4 D4
East Princes
  Street Gdns   4 C3

Edinburgh Castle   4 B4
  1. Drawbridge &
    Gatehouse
  2. Argyle & Mills
    Mount Batteries
  3. Mills Mount Barracks
  4. Governor's House
  5. St. Margarets Chapel
  6. National War
    Memorial
  7. Old Palace:
    Crown Room
    Queen Mary's Room
  8. Great Hall:
    French Prison
    Mons Meg
  9. United Services
    Museum

  10. New Barracks
  11. Hospital

Edinburgh University   5 E6
Festival Theatre   5 E5
Filmhouse   4 A5
Fire Brigade H.Q.
  & Museum   4 B5
Fire Station   4 A6
Floral Clock   4 C3
Galloping Glen   4 A6
George Heriots School   4 D5
George Square Theatre   5 E6
Georgian House   4 A2
Gladstones Land (4)   4 D3
Greyfriars Bobby Statue 4 D5
Greyfriars Kirk   4 D5
Head Post Office   5 E2
Holyrood Brewery   5 G3
Holyrood Park   5 G5
Holyroodhouse Abbey   5 H2
Hunter Building   4 C5
Huntly House The Peoples
- Story Museum (5)   5 G3
International
  Conference Centre   4 A5
John Knox's House (6)   5 F3
Lady Stairs House (7)   4 C3
Law Courts   4 D4
McEwan Hall   4 D5
Melville Museum   4 D1
Mercat Cross   4 D4
Minto House   5 E4
Moray House,
  College of Education   5 F3
Mountbatten Building   4 C5
National Gallery
  of Scotland   4 C3
National Library   4 D4
National Monument &
  Parthenon   5 F2
National Portrait Gallery &
  Museum of Antiquities 4 C1
Nelson Monument   5 F2
Nelsons College   4 A2
Observatory   5 F1
Open Air Theatre   4 B3
Outlook Tower &
  Camera Obscura   4 C4
Palace of Holyroodhouse 5 H2
Parliament House   4 D4
Playhouse Theatre   5 E1

Pleasance Theatre   5
Police H.Q.   5
Princess Alexandra
  Hospital   4
Queen Street Gdns   4
Queensberry Hospital   5
Regent Gardens   5
Regent Road Park   5
Register House   4
Reid Music School   4
Royal Infirmary   4
Royal Lyceum Theatre   4
Royal Mile
  Primary School   5
Royal Scottish Academy 4
Royal Scottish Museum 4
Royal Society
  of Edinburgh   4
St Andrews House   5
St Cuthberts Church   4
St Giles Cathedral   4
St James Centre   4
St Johns Church   4
St Mary's Cathedral   5
St Thomas of Aquins
  R. C. High School   4
Salisbury Crags   5
Scott Monument   4
Sherriff Court House   4
Simpson Memorial
  Maternity Hospital   4
Students Centre   5
Surgeons Hall   5
Swimming Pool   5
The Kings Meadow   5
The Rock Top   5
The Tron   5
Tourist Information
  Centre   4
Traverse Theatre   4
Usher Hall   4
Vehicle Pound   4
Visitors Centre   5
Waverley Market   4
Wax Museum (8)   5
Wellhouse Tower   5
West Princes
  Street Gdns   4
William Robertson
  Building   5
Youth Centre   5